Budgeting for Managers

Other titles in the Briefcase Books series include:

Customer Relationship Management by Kristin Anderson and Carol Kerr

Communicating Effectively by Lani Arredondo

Performance Management by Robert Bacal

Recognizing and Rewarding Employees by R. Brayton Bowen

Motivating Employees by Anne Bruce and James S. Pepitone

Building a High Morale Workplace by Anne Bruce

Six Sigma for Managers by Greg Brue

Leadership Skills for Managers by Marlene Caroselli

Negotiating Skills for Managers by Steven P. Cohen

Effective Coaching by Marshall J. Cook

Conflict Resolution by Daniel Dana

Project Management by Gary R. Heerkens

Managing Teams by Lawrence Holpp

Hiring Great People by Kevin C. Klinvex, Matthew S. O'Connell, and Christopher P. Klinvex

Retaining Top Employees by J. Leslie McKeown

Empowering Employees by Kenneth L. Murrell and Mimi Meredith

Presentation Skills for Managers by Jennifer Rotondo and Mike Rotondo

The Manager's Guide to Business Writing by Suzanne D. Sparks

Skills for New Managers by Morey Stettner

The Manager's Survival Guide by Morey Stettner

The Manager's Guide to Effective Meetings by Barbara J. Streibel

Interviewing Techniques for Managers by Carolyn P. Thompson

Managing Multiple Projects by Michael Tobis and Irene P. Tobis

A Briefcase Book

Budgeting for Managers

Sid Kemp
Eric Dunbar

McGraw-Hill
New York Chicago San Francisco Lisbon London
Madrid Mexico City Milan New Delhi San Juan
Seoul Singapore Sydney Toronto

The McGraw-Hill Companies

1 2 1 3 1 4 1 5 QFR/QFR 1 5 4 3

ISBN 0-07-139133-9

This is a CWL Publishing Enterprises Book, *developed and produced for McGraw-Hill by CWL Publishing Enterprises, Inc., www.cwlpub.com.*

Contents

Preface

I remember the first time I made a budget. I had just started a new job, my first time as a manager. My boss, the dean of the school, said, "Sid, we have $50,000 to spend on computer systems this year. Please prepare a budget."

Wow! All the exercises in school, all my thinking as I started the job and wrote out a plan for my work, hadn't prepared me for that. *$50,000 for my first budget.* And it was up to me to plan it well. If I did, then the computer labs for students would run well for the year, professors would be able to do research on their new computers, and—most challenging of all—I would build a network for the school's administrative staff. I don't think I need to tell you how nervous I was.

This book is written for the young manager I was then, just a few years out of college with a liberal arts degree. It's the book I wish someone had dropped into my hands on that day. It's also written for you if you're working your way up from line supervisor to manager, or if you're working day and night to make your small business succeed, or if you're setting up a new department. It will help you if your business is growing, or shrinking, or launching a new venture. Managing our money well is a key ingredient for business success.

My first budget succeeded and, three years later, I launched my own business. Since then, I've been training new managers and consulting for all kinds of businesses. I've learned a lot from my large customers, written books on best practices, and taught these methods to the new managers and small business executives who are willing to learn and want to succeed. I hope I can do the same for you.

My co-author and I were careful to include all the aspects of budgeting: income and expense, production work and projects, preparation, and presentation. We have chapters that will help you work with the accounting and finance departments if you are in a medium-sized or large company and a chapter that will help you if you're going it on your own. Whatever kind of budget you need to make, this book is for you.

Eric Dunbar, my co-author, has the training that I didn't have. He has an M.B.A. and excels at setting up financial systems for small businesses. I learned while flying by the seat of my pants, while he learned in more formal settings. Together, we've put together a realistic, practical book that is also precise and clear. It's now in your hands.

Please do more than read this book. Work with it. Set up your budget next to our examples and try out all the ideas. A lot of creative thinking goes into making a good budget: we want you to do your best in your own way, while learning from those who specialize in accounting and finance.

A budget is more than just numbers; it supports success and teamwork for you and your department. In preparing your department's budget, you secure the funds and resources your team needs to succeed. In managing the money and allowing your team to make spending decisions with you, you empower your team to plan well, work well together, and succeed.

Your team's success is yours, and success for your company as well.

Special Features

The idea behind the books in the Briefcase Series is to give you practical information written in a friendly, person-to-person style. The chapters are short, deal with tactical issues, and include lots of examples. They also feature numerous boxes designed to give you different types of specific information. Here's a description of the boxes you'll find in this book.

These boxes are designed to give you tips and tactics that will help you more effectively implement the methods described in this book.

These boxes provide warnings for where things could go wrong when you're undertaking your budget.

These boxes highlight insider tips for taking advantage of the practices you'll learn about in this book.

Every subject has its special jargon and terms. These boxes provide definitions of these concepts.

It's always important to have examples of what others have done, either well or not so well. Find such stories in these boxes.

This identifies boxes where you'll find specific procedures you can follow to take advantage of the book's advice.

How can you make sure you won't make a mistake when dealing with a problem? You can't, but these boxes will give you practical advice on how to minimize the possibility.

Acknowledgments

My deepest appreciation goes to Eric Dunbar, my co-author, for all I have learned from him in our year of working together; to Kari Richter, for her excellent copy editing and fast turnaround; and to the staff of CWL Publishing Enterprises for their clarity, support, and swift, high-quality work.

I also wish to thank my many clients and friends who have helped me develop these ideas and put them into practice over the years.

Lastly, my wife, Kristen H. Lindbeck, and my mother, Edie Kemp, were extremely patient and supportive as I wrote this book.

About the Authors

Sid Kemp is a trainer and consultant, and the author of several books in the *Project Success*™ management series. He is a successful entrepreneur dedicated to learning the best practices of *Fortune* 500 companies and other industry leaders, improving them, and making them available to mid-level and entry-level managers and to owners and managers of small businesses.

Sid's company, Quality Technology & Instruction, L.L.C., offers keynote speaking, training, consulting, facilitation, coaching, and workshops to managers in business, the non-profit sector, and government. QTI's mission is to help our customers succeed by helping them do their work in the best way possible and to introduce methods of win/win success to the business community.

QTI operates from the *Partnering Perspective*™, creating teams of experts who deliver higher quality than anyone could do alone. And each team member grows by participating in success. We succeed along with our customers. In the spirit of partnering, Sid has co-authored a number of books with others, bringing their expertise to readers.

Sid always enjoys talking to his readers, helping them, and learning from them. You can reach him by e-mail at sid@qualitytechnology.com or learn more about the services his company offers at www.qualitytechnology.com.

Eric Dunbar, M.B.A., J.D., is an expert at setting up financial systems for small businesses. He is gifted in explaining accounting practices and issues to managers. Eric contributed his expertise to every chapter of this book; he made sure that the terminology was correct and also that all the numbers added up.

Eric brings a wealth of management experience to this book, not only from his work at QTI, but also from managing a private investigation firm and working as a legal intern for a prestigious private firm. He holds a degree in law from Seattle University and an M.B.A. in international business and a B.B.A. in accounting from University of Texas at San Antonio.

Budgeting for Managers

1

Budgeting: Why and How

Act before there is a problem.
Bring order before there is disorder.
—Lao Tzu

Budgeting is more than just a job we have to get done to satisfy the financial department. Planning and budgeting can help us lead our team to success. Sometimes, when we write a plan, we catch errors. It's a lot better to catch errors in a plan than to have problems later on in the office or on the shop floor because you didn't catch the errors. In fact, it's been shown that good planning will typically reduce the costs of a project by about a factor of 10.

In this chapter, you will learn how to create a simple expense budget. There's a lot here, but don't worry. Every idea in this chapter will be explained further on in the book in more detail. Our goal for this chapter is to create a simple success together: your first budget. Let's go!

Key Term

Plan A written document describing what you are going to do to achieve a goal. It usually includes the steps involved and a timeline for completion.

Budget A plan that includes the money you will spend and when you will spend it. In addition to expenses, a budget can also include income.

Team The people who work with or under you to achieve a goal you all share. It doesn't matter if your organization calls them a team, a department, or anything else. What matters is that you will support and guide these people, all of you will work together, and all of you will deliver the results the organization wants.

Why Make a Budget? Who Reads Budgets?

There are several good reasons to create a budget and to make it a good one. The reasons are tied to the people who will read and use the budget. Each reader will look at the budget in a different way and do something different with it. If you know your readers, you can make a budget that will impress everyone—and, more important, show how your group is contributing to the organization and therefore approve the funds you need to proceed. If you know how the budget will be used, you will know how to write it in an easy-to-use way. More important, it will help you succeed and show that you are a good manager and that your team is doing a good job. So, let's take a look at your audiences and what they will do with your budget.

You and Your Team

You and your team are your first, and most important, audience for your work plans and your budget. When you read the budget, you want it to make sense. This means that you understand it, of course, but it means more than that. The budget should be believable and workable and it should work the way your team works and be appropriate to your situation.

Your Boss

Your boss is your second audience. Of course, you want the budget to be correct, clear, and complete for him or her. If your boss checks your work closely, you don't want any errors to show up. If your boss doesn't check it closely, you certainly don't want the budget to go further upstairs with mistakes in it. Your boss will also check the totals of the budget against available funds. In some companies and in many government agencies, the boss will also check the budget against rules and limitations. Some organizations require that top managers approve the line-item budget.

A Budget That Works

Nicolai was planning the budget for supplies for a small manufacturing shop. The parts he needed to buy were cheaper by the caseload than by the box. But Nicolai's shop didn't have much warehouse space, so he chose to buy a few boxes at a time, instead of a whole caseload. He spent more on the parts, but he was working within the space he had. The extra money he spent on the parts was worth it, because it saved the cost of renting a larger space to store the parts.

Your boss will also seek or approve funds for the budget. In a company, you may do work for another department, and then bill that department for the work you do. Or the cost may be billed to a client, but your boss will need to make sure that you are planning to spend the right amount of money for that client. Some of the money may come from restricted funds, such as a training budget or government grants. Then you can

Line-item budget A budget where the name of each line is set, as is the amount of money you can spend on each item. If you must work with a line-item budget, and it specifies $1,000 for training materials and $500 for office supplies, you can't spend $1,100 on training materials and $400 on office supplies. The authority to move money from one line to another must be granted at a higher level.

Block budget The opposite of a line-item budget. You are given a block of money. You present the details of your plan in line items. But, later on, if you want to spend more on training and less on office supplies, you are free to do so. As long as you don't overspend the block of money before the end of the year, the money is under your control.

> **Key Term**
> **Restricted funds** Money that you can use, but only for a specific purpose or with specific limitations or requirements.

use that money only for the purpose specified in the budget. You will have to track this money carefully and you may have to work with other restrictions on the funds, such as using particular types of contracts or submitting receipts that prove how the money was spent.

Three other audiences for your budget are the financial department, the accounting department, and, possibly, the human resources department.

The Financial Department

The financial department is responsible for acquiring and planning for the use of all funds within your company. The budget you put together becomes part of the whole corporate budget they create. If your company has an annual report, your plan and budget will appear as a part of the total financial picture. If you deliver a clear budget with no errors, you make their work easier—as well as your own, because you won't have to correct it later on. If your team gets its work done well within your budget, you improve the company's bottom line and help ensure success.

The Accounting Department

The accounting department is responsible for managing and tracking all financial transactions for the company. They will create account codes for each of your line items and assign them in their computer system. Every time money is approved or spent, they will track that event and take from the money allocated in your budget and show it as actually spent.

> **Key Term**
> **Allocated** Assigned to be spent for a particular purpose. If your budget is accepted, this means that the money has been allocated for the purposes listed in your budget. Money is usually allocated for use within a particular year.

> **The Unexpected Raise**
>
> Juanita prepared a departmental budget for a year that includes a salary for a current team member of $36,000 per year, or $3,000 per month. It looked fine to her. When human resources checked it, they noticed that since each employee gets an annual raise on the anniversary of his or her starting date and this employee started in August, the 5% raise would make the budget off by $150 per month for the last five months of the year. With the help of human resources, Juanita adjusted the salary to $3,150 per month for August through December and the annual budget for that line item to $36,750.

The Human Resources Department

If your budget includes money to pay salaries for you or your team, it will also involve the human resources department, sometimes called personnel. People in human resources work closely with accounting and finance with regard to salary and other employee-related expenses. You should ask them to check your budget in relation to salaries.

Creating an accurate, workable plan and budget allows your team to get the money it needs from finance, keep track of it with accounting and human resources, and succeed. You can succeed only with a good budget. The success of your team or department within your budget looks good for your team, for you, and for your boss. It also helps the bottom line of your organization.

Eight Steps to Creating a Budget

Now that you know your audience, you're ready to begin tackling your first budget. As you work through this section, take your time and make sure that you get a basic understanding of the ideas. If anything is too complicated right now, don't worry. It will show up in more detail in the next 11 chapters.

Choosing Where to Start

There are two basic starting points for a budget. We can look either at what we did before or at what we are planning to do. In

> **For Example**
>
> ### A Fresh Start
>
> Evan was the new marketing manager for a small company. Up until now, he had always made his budgets starting from what was actually spent in the last two years. But he discovered that this company had done almost no marketing in the past two years because it had three large clients and wasn't looking for new work. Now things have changed. Evan was hired because two of the clients went out of business and the company now needs more marketing. Evan sat down with the company owner and asked him what the marketing goals for the company were for the next year. With the owner's help, he built an accurate marketing plan to meet those goals. Then, starting with the plan instead of the prior year's spending, he made a budget that would allow him to allocate funds more realistically.

the first option, we review a prior year or years and then make changes where we think the future will be different from the past. In the second option, we look at a written plan of what we are going to do and ask, "What will I need to buy? How much money will I have to spend?"

Both approaches are good and you can start with either one. However, if you don't have accurate information about the prior year or you know that this year is going to be very different, then you have to work from a plan, rather than from past results. To make a really good budget, it's best to look at the budget both ways.

Suppose that you have good, actual expense figures from at least one prior year. Does that mean that it's best to start from them? Not necessarily. Sometimes, it's still better to start from your work plan for the new year. This depends a lot on how much production work you do and how much project work you do.

When you're creating a budget for production work, you're probably better off starting from last year's budget. If you'll be working in much the same way, then last year's plan is a good start for this year's plan. However, when you're creating a budget for a project, you're better off starting with your project plan. Because projects are unique, something you've done before is not a good model. Build from your plan so that your budget

> **Smart Managing**
>
> **Actual Not Estimated**
>
> If you're building your budget from a past year's budget, make sure that you base it on actual spending, not estimates. Check with accounting to make sure that the figures from last year are accurate and that nothing was left out. Also, think about whether there should be any new categories or line items in this year's budget, then add them, rather than trying to squeeze your new budget into an old plan. You'll probably change the amounts of each line item—that's what estimating is all about—but you'll also want to add or change the names of line items if you have a good reason to do so.

describes what you actually need to buy, hire, or acquire to succeed on the project. Your budget may be broken into different parts and each part can be done either way—based on the past or on the plan. In this chapter we'll discuss the basics of creating a budget from last year's budget. Creating a project plan and budget is covered in Chapter 5.

> **Key Term**
>
> **Production work** Any work done in much the same way over and over again. Running an assembly line and processing insurance claims forms are good examples of production work.
>
> **Project** A temporary endeavor undertaken to create a unique product or service. In a project, you are doing work just once, not repeating it. Building a new assembly line or installing a new computer system to handle insurance claims forms are good examples of projects.

Creating a New Budget from an Old One: Step by Step

In this section, we will create a simple expense budget for this year from a prior year. Later in the book, you will learn to budget income and other elements and to work with several years of information at once. All of the ideas presented briefly here will be explained again with a lot more detail in later chapters.

Step 1: Gathering Information

The first job is to gather accurate information about the past. This is not always easy. Sometimes, records are not kept well. Often, we need to project next year's budget before this year is

For Example

Production and Projects

Robert is the manager of an information technology department, which keeps all of the computers running and also installs new systems. In planning for the coming year, there are three big parts to his budget: support, providing computers for new staff, and installing a new warehouse inventory system.

For the support plan, he builds his budget based on last year's budget, because he expects support for next year to be pretty much like last year. To purchase and install computers for new staff, he talks to HR and learns how many people will be hired each month and which ones will need computers. Then he builds a plan to provide computers before the new employees start work and writes a budget for that project plan. Then he consults with the vendor who's providing the warehouse inventory system and creates a project plan and a budget.

Line items in his budget may be a combination of all three parts. For example, the figure for the cost of new computers would include new computers to replace old ones from support, new computers for new staff, and new computers for the warehouse.

over or before the information on this year's expenses is ready. Sometimes, we can find out what we spent, but we can't get the answer to the magic question: Why?

For now, let's say that we manage to gather information on what we spent last year. Our example is a budget for the

Tricks of the Trade

Using a Spreadsheet Program

A spreadsheet program can take a lot of the tedium out of creating a budget. If you know the basics of a spreadsheet program, it will take care of addition, subtraction, and simple percentage increases for you. Later in this book, we'll show you how to have the spreadsheet program check your work for you as well. Many managers take the time to learn advanced spreadsheet functions by taking two or three days of classes or by reading a book and working through the exercises.

There are three popular spreadsheet programs available. Microsoft Excel™ is packaged with Microsoft Office™, so it's probably the most available. Microsoft Works™ contains a spreadsheet tool that is good enough for simple budgets and costs a good deal less. And some companies use Lotus 1-2-3™, which is just as good as Excel for everything you will need to do in a budget.

photocopy department ("the print shop") of a medium-sized company (Table 1-1). It's January 2003 and we need to create an expense budget for the year.

Print Shop Expenses	2002 Actual	2003 Estimated
Equipment leases	$3,600	
Toner	900	
Plain paper	300	
Special papers	60	
Equipment purchase	600	
Service contracts	1,500	
Equipment repair	350	
Miscellaneous	150	
Sales tax	142	
Total Expenses	$7,602	

Table 1-1. Print shop expenses (2002)

Step 2: Understanding Each Line

Preparing a good budget is detail work. We need to do more than say, "I guess we'll spend the same next year." We need to know why we spent what we did and think about what will change. So we examine each line and, using our own memory, meetings with others, and reviews of receipts and contracts, we understand *why* we spent what we did.

For example, why did we spend $3,600 on equipment leases? A check of the lease contracts shows that all three machines are on a five-year lease-purchase plan at $100 per month. Why did we spend $300 on plain paper? We can check purchase orders, inventories, and copier counters and discover that we made about 5,000 copies per month, which used 10 reams of paper at a cost of about $25. We ask similar questions about each line item.

Keeping Budget Notes Throughout the Year

Plan ahead. Whenever you approve a major expense, make a note of why the expense was necessary. It's easiest to keep all these notes in one computer file. You could put them in a word processing document called, for example, "2003 budget notes." Or, if you prefer spreadsheets, you can use the feature that attaches little notes to each cell. Either way, when you sit down to make your next budget, you'll know why you spent money the way you did. In a large organization, you can review the budget monthly and ask people why large expenses occurred and make your notes.

Step 3: Predicting the Future

Unless you have a *working* crystal ball, the best way to predict the future is to picture it, meet with people about what they want and what's happening, and then make an estimated or calculated guess. Your guess will be the best one possible because it's based on good information, your own experience, careful thinking, and accurate calculations.

New managers are often afraid of writing down a lot of guesses and giving them to their boss. That's understandable. But that's all anybody ever does when predicting the future. Reasonable and calculated guesses are the best we can do for budgeting. Even Alan Greenspan, when talking about when the economy will improve, is just making an estimated and calculated guess, based on his team's research and experience. It won't be comfortable at first. But, if you follow the steps carefully and thoughtfully, you'll be surprised how often you'll be right or close, as long as you understand how your office works.

Let's look at some sample line items and see what it's like to predict the future. In examining the lease contracts, you realize that two of the machines have been on lease for only two years and you'll pay another $1,200 on each of them this next year. But the third machine is now five years old and has a purchase option. For $350, it's yours. Since it works fine, you decide to buy it. You can now predict lease expenses for 2003: two machines at $1,200 each for $2,400. And you add $350 to the equipment expense line so you can purchase the third copier.

Doing this makes you think about service contracts, so you check. The two machines under five years old will have service contracts with renewal options at the same rate, of $500 each per year. The service company you've been using won't support machines over five years old. You ask around and a friend tells you that there's a local repair shop that services older machines. You arrange a service contract with them for the old machine at $600 per year. So, you budget $1,600 for service contracts in 2003.

> **Accurate Self-Assessment** (Tricks of the Trade)
>
> Expert managers understand the difference between what they know and what they don't know. It's essential to know if there's missing information or if something isn't clear. It is better to say honestly, "We spent $3,000 on supplies last year, but we lost track of $600," than to try to hide that fact. We learn best by being honest about the problem or our lack of knowledge and resolving to learn more and to do better next time.

Now that we've planned the equipment budget, let's take a look at supplies. We use up supplies to support our rate of production. For a copy shop, the key rate is the number of copies a month and, in our example, almost all of that is plain paper copying. In 2002, the copy shop averaged 5,000 copies per month. Will it be different this year?

The best people to answer that question are your customers. You could go to the manager or assistant manager or secretary of each department and ask them if they are likely to want more copies than last year, or less, or the same. When you add up the numbers, you will have your estimate for production levels, so you can estimate your expenses.

So, checking in with each customer, we discover that we will probably make 72,000 copies this coming year, instead of 60,000, an increase of 20%. How does this information help you estimate your budget?

The number of copies determines the amount of plain paper and toner that you buy. So, we can increase these by 20%.

Smart Managing

Partner with Your Customers

Help your customers think about what they need from you. You might tell them, "Last year, you made 12,000 copies. It looks like 8,000 of them were for two big mailings." Then you can add questions to get them thinking: How many mailings are you doing this year? Is your mailing list growing? Are you doing anything else that will require photocopies?

Helping them think through their needs will not only give you a more accurate budget and make it easier to plan your team's workload, it will also help them appreciate you more. Of course, it's also important to respect your customers' time. If a customer would prefer that you just send a quick e-mail and let her reply, that's fine, too.

Putting in these figures, we now get a projection for 2003 that looks like Table 1-2:

Print Shop Expenses	2002 Actual	2003 Estimated
Equipment leases	$3,600	$2,400
Toner	900	1,080
Plain paper	300	360
Special papers	60	
Equipment purchase	600	950
Service contracts	1,500	1,600
Equipment repair	350	
Miscellaneous	150	
Sales tax	142	
Total expenses	$7,602	$6,390

Table 1-2. Print shop expenses (part of 2003)

Step 4: Reviewing the Results

Looking at our estimate (Table 1-2), we see that we've got a new figure for every line item that cost over $500 last year. It's time to ask ourselves some questions before we finish up the budget.

Budget Review Checklist

- **Does it make sense?** For each item, do the numbers look right? Think about the decision you've made and make sure you're comfortable with it. If not, then get someone's opinion or rethink it yourself.
- **Does it add up?** Even if you use a computerized spreadsheet, you'll want to check your numbers.
- **Are the big items right?** Pay more attention to the line items with higher figures. If any aren't done, finish those first, using the same methods you used in Step 3.

Step 5: Finishing the Budget

Once you complete the larger line items, you need to finish up the smaller ones. In our example, it doesn't matter too much how you do it. Even if every one of the four unfinished items on our budget doubled for 2003, it would only add $702 to the budget and the total budget would still be smaller than last year.

On your own budget, total up the smaller items. All together, they may be more than half of the budget. In that case, you'll need to spend some time planning them carefully. On the other hand, the small items may add up to a tiny part of your budget, which isn't worth much of your time. This allows you some flexibility to think about how people view your budget and your team. If the "bean counters" like to see level costs, keep the numbers the same. If they expect reasonable growth, then use a growth figure similar to the one used for the big items. If they tend to accept budgets at the beginning of the year, but make it very hard to allocate extra money later in the year, then put in higher numbers to give yourself a little leeway.

Bean counter Someone in finance or accounting. The term is sometimes friendly and sometimes derogatory, so be careful how you use it. Most often, the term implies that a person is more interested in accounts and making the numbers look good than in using the money for the things you feel you need to do your work.

In our case, we're going to assume that the small supply items are going to increase along with the large ones, at 20%. But we have no reason to think repair costs will go up. We're nearly finished. The only line left is for sales tax. The sales tax line is a bit different from the other lines, because it is based on a calculation using the figures from other lines. We can add up any line items that require sales tax and multiply the results by the local sales tax percentage. (State laws vary on which items are taxed.) If you're working with a spreadsheet, you can simply enter a formula to perform this calculation for you. In Table 1-3, those line items are in italics. To make it interesting, let's say that last year sales tax was 6%, but this year it's increasing to 8%.

Print Shop Expenses	2002 Actual	2003 Estimated
Equipment leases	$3,600	$2,400
Toner	*900*	*1,080*
Plain paper	*300*	*360*
Special papers	*60*	*72*
Equipment purchase	*600*	*950*
Service contracts	1,500	1,600
Equipment repair	*350*	*350*
Miscellaneous	*150*	*180*
Sales tax	**142**	**239**
Total expenses	$7,602	$7,231

Table 1-3. Print shop expenses (items with sales tax in italic)

Take a look at the sales tax line (in bold). In 2002, sales tax was 6% of the total of the six taxable line items in italics. In 2003, we use the new figures for each line, and we use the new tax rate of 8%. Take a moment to copy these numbers into your own spreadsheet or to use a calculator and check the figures. (If I made a mistake, send me an e-mail!)

Step 6: Adding Budgetary Assumptions

A budget is more than just numbers. Your sources of informa-

> **Taxable item** A line item that is subject to sales or some other tax. A line item may be subject to sales tax in one situation and not in another. For example, if you buy supplies for internal use in a business, they are taxable. If you buy the same item to produce items for sale, you can make a tax-exempt purchase. And, if you work for a not-for-profit organization, then almost all purchases are tax-exempt. Whether an item is taxable or not also varies from state to state. For example, in the print shop budget, repair services were taxable. In other states, repairs are broken into parts (taxable) and service (not taxable).

tion and reasoning are important as well. With this information, you and others can review the budget, improve it, and easily extend it into the future. And, if errors appear, it's possible to trace the source of the mistakes. Perhaps your planning was right, but you were given the wrong information to begin with.

> **Budgetary assumptions** A short document that answers the questions:
> - Where did you get your numbers?
> - What thinking led you to this estimate?

We put all this information into a one- or two-page document called *budgetary assumptions* (Table 1-4). Keep it short and simple. Also, make sure it is clear so that you can remem-

Print Shop Budgetary Assumptions

General: Year 2002 figures were provided by the accounting department using year-end actual results.

Line item

Equipment leases: Costs lowered because one of three units will be purchased in 1/2003.

Equipment purchase: Increase due to execution of buy option on leased photocopy machine

All supply items: 20% increase based on discussions with customers about expected growth in demand for services.

Sales tax: Calculated as 6% of total taxable items in 2002. Due to rate increase, calculated at 8% of total taxable items in 2003

Table 1-4. The print shop: budgetary assumptions

ber and explain all your ideas later if you need to.

This document is brief but clear. Not all items are explained, only the most important ones, that is, the ones that changed most or the ones that were based on new rules. Yet this is enough information to make it easy to evaluate and improve your budget throughout the year and to make it even easier to prepare a budget next year.

Step 7: Checking Your Work

You are almost ready to present your budget. But you are probably a bit nervous—and you should be! You don't want to have someone else find your mistakes after you've delivered your budget. So, the best thing is to find those mistakes now and have someone else help you do it.

You need to do more than check your numbers. Capitalization, spelling, punctuation, and grammar are also important. And it never hurts to take a few extra minutes to make a document look good with stylish, professional fonts and formatting. Chapter 6 will guide you through checking your work and Chapter 7 will show you how to make a professional budget presentation.

TRICKS OF THE TRADE

Learn from the Old-Timers

Most of us may not remember when budgets were done by hand. In those days, mistakes were a lot harder to find. And, strangely enough, there were fewer of them. Having computers makes things so easy that, sometimes, we become lazy or sloppy.

My mother used to project student enrollment for every school in Philadelphia. A co-worker would help her proofread tables by reading every number aloud from the original while she checked the new version. It was a lot of work, but it led to award-winning results.

It's very hard to catch our own errors. We tend to see what we *think* we wrote. We assume that our spreadsheets are working the way we want them to and we miss errors created by bad formulas. To prevent this, work with a partner. Have someone unfamiliar with your work read it aloud while you verify it. If no one on your team is available, help another manager with his or her budget in return for getting help with yours.

Step 8: Delivering Your Budget

Back at the beginning of this chapter, we discussed the different audiences for your budget. You may well present your budget differently to each audience. (Of course, the numbers should always be the same.)

With your team, focus on how you came up with the figures and how you expect the team to spend money and track expenses through the year. Help them be responsible about tracking money and let them know you support them in having what they need to do their job.

Your manager is likely to want to go over the budget carefully before it goes to accounting and finance. It's good to make the time to sit down with him or her and review your assumptions. Your manager may also want to change some items. For example, if your manager knows that accounting routinely cuts each item by 10%, it may be wise to increase your numbers so you can get what you need.

The financial department may or may not want to see your budgetary assumptions. Some financial departments will not want to see all of your notes but will want certain very specific items. Ask them for their guidelines and samples of the terminology they want you to use. Much of what the financial department prepares is available to stockholders or even the general public; you'll want to follow their lead in presenting information appropriately when it goes outside the company.

Account codes The numbers assigned to expense categories or jobs so that the budget can be tracked throughout the year. We'll discuss them further in Chapter 2.

Accounting will probably not want to see the budgetary assumptions page. They will want to put the numbers into the computerized accounting system. If they've given you account codes, you'll want to deliver your estimates for the new year with those numbers, to make it easy for them to set up the new year on their system.

Success Review

We've made a really good budget. What makes it good?

- It's written clearly, so that anyone can understand it.
- It is based on good information from our customers and our own experience.
- We started with last year's actual expenses, but we also did some planning for the coming year.
- We researched the most important items and made some good management choices, such as buying the old copier.

In preparing our budget, we've set up our team for a year of success.

There's a lot more to learn. In Chapter 2, we'll look at all the parts of a budget and learn to forecast income. In Chapters 3 and 4, we'll expand on what we did here, so you can create a complete production budget. In Chapter 5, you'll learn how to create a simple project plan and budget. After that, we'll look at presenting your budget, tracking money through the year, and some advanced topics, such as budgeting for small businesses. Even if you thought you weren't that good with numbers, you'll probably find it easy to learn if you go step by step and work out each exercise as you go.

Manager's Checklist for Chapter 1

- ❑ Having a good plan and a budget reduces costs by helping you take care of things before they become problems.
- ❑ A good budget is made up of accurate information, thoughtful predictions, good guesswork, and careful calculations.
- ❑ Any budget contains guesswork. If this makes you nervous, just remember that, if you have good facts and think clearly, your guesses will be as good as anyone else's—probably better.
- ❑ You can create a budget from past data or from future plans. If you're doing production work, you're repeating past work,

so past data is a good place to start. If you're working on a project, then it's better to start from your plan. Either way, check your budget using both approaches.

- ❑ Follow the eight-step plan to creating a budget and you'll create a budget that will help your team succeed and help financing, accounting, and other departments get their work done and work with you.

2

The Parts of a Budget

The whole is greater than the sum of its parts.
—popular saying

In Chapter 1, we introduced an expense budget for a single year. Now, we will look at the bigger picture of budgeting. In the first section, we'll look at shorter-term (monthly) and longer-term (multi-year) budgets and how they link together. In the next section, we'll look at how the work you plan to do is the best source of information for your budget. Then, we'll take a look at forecasting income. We'll close the chapter by introducing some terms and concepts from accounting. You don't need to know accounting to be a good manager and to prepare a good budget for your department. But it's always easier to use good ideas when we can, and accounting offers us some good ideas for ways to make budgets.

Time Periods of Your Budget

Time is a very important consideration in good budgeting. Do we want to plan the budget for days, weeks, months, or years?

Although budgeting for days and weeks can be useful in a household, in business we work mostly with months and years. So we'll start there.

> **Short-term budget** Any budget up to one year long.
>
> **Long-term budget** Any budget over a year long.
>
> **Accounting year** A one-year period starting in a particular month, not necessarily January, used for business accounting.

Budgets for a year or less are usually called *short-term* budgets, and those for over a year are *long term*. One good reason for thinking in terms of a year is that many things tend to repeat on an annual cycle. Another is that companies file tax forms annually, so it's good to keep track of what we are doing according to accounting years.

> **The Accounting Year for a Seasonal Business**
>
> A business with most of its sales during the Christmas season probably won't want to end its accounting year in December. That would require too much accounting work when sales are heavy. It also would break up the big season (which includes after-Christmas and New Year's sales) into two years. The company might choose an accounting year that begins on April 1 and ends on March 31, after winter sales are over. Corporate taxes are due two and a half months after the end of the business year. So, if the year ends March 31, the corporate taxes are due May 15.

A short-term budget has two purposes: planning and control. We plan for what money we'll receive and how we'll spend or save the money we get. We also want to be able to control the money we receive and spend. We control money by tracking actual results against estimates and taking action to resolve any important discrepancies.

> **Tracking** Comparing actual results against the estimates we made in our budget and noting the differences.
>
> **Control** Taking corrective action based on tracking, changing the way we work to get the results we want.

Long-term budgets are only for planning; they are

Smart Managing

What to Do with a Difference

When we find that the amount of money we actually spent is different from our estimates, this doesn't mean that anything is wrong. Things may, indeed, be very right. If our copy shop bought more paper this month, it may be that we made more copies. Since customers paid for them, that means our business is growing! When actual and estimated figures differ, the experienced manager asks, "Why?" If the actual business results are good, then the only question is "Can we do a better job estimating next time?" On the other hand, the comparison may show us problems. Perhaps someone placed a double order by mistake. Or perhaps another department is borrowing paper and not returning it. Once we know *why* the discrepancy is there, then we can decide *what*, if anything, we should do.

not for control. Our best guess for our income and expenses the year after next or three or five years from now is not likely to be as good as the one we'll make just before the beginning of that year. We prepare the long-term budget so that we can plan ahead and prepare for what we think will happen. And we refine and revise it as we get closer.

The short-term and long-term plans and budgets are related. Today's decision can make a difference for a long time to come. The total cost (or total benefit) of a decision has to be considered, not only the results for the current budget year.

CAUTION!

Saving Money Isn't Always a Good Thing

A food processing plant had a huge grain elevator that was designed to work around the clock all year, with one week off each year for maintenance. The company decided to save money and increase production by skipping annual maintenance. It did this for five years, until the elevator quit working altogether.

When the repairman came, he found that the main drive shaft was cracked. This never would have happened if annual maintenance had been performed. The damage was so bad that someone could have been killed. Fortunately, no one was injured. But the repair costs and lost production time cost far more than the money saved by skipping scheduled downtime over the last five years.

Budget and Vision

In this section we'll talk about one of the best things a manager can do and one of the worst mistakes we could make.

The best thing to do is to bring vision to your planning process. To have a vision means to see what you will do, to picture it ahead of time. Some companies have statements of vision, mission, and values. If yours does, that is the best place to start. Plan the work of your department to match the vision of the business. Then, plan a budget to meet that vision.

What do you do if your organization has no written vision statement? Every organization has a vision, even when it's not written. Talk to your boss or read articles written by senior executives at your company. Read the annual report to stockholders. Do senior people at the company talk about customer service? Do they talk about competition and increasing their share of the market? Do they talk about cost saving and efficiency? That will give you an idea of the company's image for management and their vision of what they want it to be.

What is the one thing you don't want to do? Don't think, "New numbers come from old numbers." For example, it would be a mistake to think, "We had about $50,000 in sales every December for the last three years, so I guess we'll do $50,000 again next December." Each year's sales come from the products, marketing, and sales efforts of that year. This year might be different. Sales results, and every other dollar fig-

> **Sharing a Vision with Your Team**
>
> Smart Managing
>
> Just as an organization should have a vision, you may decide that your team should have one as well. A good vision is short and simple. It could be, for example, "Make every customer smile." You can encourage a positive attitude and focus your team on doing good work without rocking the boat. And you can change the focus from time to time. Maybe you used "Make every customer smile" for the big Christmas sales season. Now, you're struggling to get through the summer doldrums, so you go for "Make every penny count."

ure in a company, come from the work we do and from the actions we take. So, find out what your department will be doing and base your budget on that.

Short Term

If we want to build a short-term budget, we might look just one month or three months ahead, but it's probably good to plan for an entire year. Table 2-1 shows a simple annual budget with monthly, quarterly, and yearly figures.

	Month	Quarter (month x 3)	Year (month x 12)
Income			
Sales	$1,250	$3,750	$15,000
Expenses			
Equipment leases	150	450	1,800
Toner	10	30	120
Plain paper	10	30	120
Special papers	15	45	180
Equipment purchase	100	300	300
Service contracts	75	225	900
Equipment repair	25	75	300
Miscellaneous	7	21	72
Sales tax	109	327	1,308
Total Expenses	$501	$1,503	$6,012
Net Income	$749	$2,247	$8,988

Table 2-1. Simple budget for a month, a quarter, and a year

This budget is not very realistic. What are the odds that you will do the same amount of work in a copy shop in August, when everyone is on vacation, as in September, when everyone is back and preparing the Christmas marketing campaign? This example just shows the basic idea of months, quarters, and years. You will want to make estimates for each month, and then show the quarters as the sum of every three months, rather than just multiplying the figures for one month times three. We'll show an example of an annual budget with variable months in Chapter 4.

Long Term

A long-term budget looks further ahead. What will your department be doing for the next five, 10, or 20 years? It may be hard to imagine. But thinking that far ahead is part of being a good manager and making a good budget.

If the copy shop needs to buy new copiers every five to seven years, it would be best to know what years we're likely to need to do so. That way, we can say, "Three years from now, we'll need a new copier." That's a lot better than not planning ahead. If we don't plan, we could find that we suddenly need to buy a new copier next month and we didn't plan for it when we made the budget for the year.

Table 2-2 shows a simplified long-term budget. Take a look at it, and then we will explain the terms and the thinking that helped us look 20 years ahead.

	1 Year	5 Years	10 Years	20 Years
Income				
Sales	$15,000	$75,000	$150,000	$300,000
Gross Income	$15,000	$75,000	$150,000	$300,000
Expenses				
Fixed Costs				
Fixed Annual	8,925	44,625	89,250	178,500
Start-up	1,000	3,000	3,000	3,000
Interim	—	—	4,000	6,000
Total Fixed Costs	$9,925	$47,625	$96,250	$187,500
Expenses				
Variable Costs				
Annual	800	4,700	9,800	19,500
Project	—	2,500	2,500	7,500
Total Variable Costs	$800	$7,200	$12,300	$27,000
Expenses				
Semi-Variable Costs				
Fixed Base/Variable Volume	1,000	7,000	12,000	25,000
Total Expenses	$11,725	$61,825	$120,550	$239,500
Net Income	$3,275	$13,175	$29,450	$60,500

Table 2-2. Simple long-term budget

Key Term

Fixed Cost A cost that does not vary year to year. From an accounting perspective, a cost that does not change even if the amount of production changes.

Fixed Annual Cost A fixed cost that is the same every year throughout the entire budget.

Start-up Cost A fixed cost that appears only in the first year or years of the budget.

Interim Cost A fixed cost that appears during a period in the middle of the budget.

Variable Cost A line item where the cost varies in different years. In accounting terms, costs that vary with the amount of production.

Annual Variable Cost A variable cost estimated as different each year.

Project Cost A variable cost calculated from a project plan.

Semi-Variable Cost A single line item calculated with a combination of fixed and variable elements.

Fixed Base/Variable Volume Cost A semi-variable cost that has a fixed component plus a variable component based on volume.

Let's look at this budget line by line. For sales income, we used the simple solution: we multiplied one year's estimated income by five, 10, and 20. We'll look at more accurate ways of forecasting income in the next section.

We broke up expenses by the different ways we might try to calculate long-term estimates. When you do this, ask which of these methods is the best choice for each type of expense: fixed, variable, or semi-variable.

Let's take a look at how we estimated each line of the expense budget.

Fixed annual costs. These expenses come from one of two sources. They can be known expenses determined by contract, such as mortgages, service contracts, or equipment leases. The other possibility is that the costs are actually variable, but neither growing nor shrinking, just varying by month and averaging out over a year or two. In our example, we calculated the annual figure from a record of the monthly expenses for the past two years shown in Table 2-3. As you see in the table, monthly figures varied from as low as zero to as high as $1,800. But, over time, things average out. We used the average of the 24 months multiplied by 12 (for 12 months in a year) as the figure for our fixed annual expenses for one year. We then multiplied this by five, 10, and 20 for those columns in Table 2-2. Any one year might vary from the average, perhaps as much as $2,000. But if our assumption that this cost is staying the same overall is true, then our longer-term projections are likely to be on target.

Copy costs	Jan	Feb	Mar	Apr	May	Jun	Jul	Aug	Sep	Oct	Nov	Dec	Year Total	2 Year Avg
2001	800	200	0	750	1,250	250	650	1,150	1,500	600	200	150	7,500	
2002	650	1,500	1,200	1,100	500	600	750	1,250	1,800	250	500	250	10,350	
													17,850	$8,925

Table 2-3. Variable averaging over months

Start-up costs. Our start-up costs were $1,000 a year for just the first three years. We see the $1,000 in the first year. We see $3,000 in the five-year column because it is a total of what we will spend for that item in all of the first five years. It shows up again in the columns for 10-year and 20-year totals. This illustrates an important fact: the five-, 10-, and 20-year columns are totals for all those years, not estimates for just the fifth, 10th, and 20th years. As a result, on this spreadsheet, as you move across a row, numbers should never go down. The next column is always the previous column plus any new income or expenses for the following years.

Interim costs. These are fixed annual costs that will appear for some years in a row and then disappear. In this case, we're predicting an extra expense of $1,000 per year for six years running, years seven through 12 of our budget. Our office has locations in six cities and the company has announced a plan to renovate facilities one city at a time, from 2009 through 2014. None of this cost appears in the first five years, four years of it are included by year 10, and all six years appear in the 20-year column.

Variable costs. These are costs that change from year to year. We may just be showing a cost that we think will vary year by year or we may be estimating costs based on a project plan.

Annual variable costs. These are costs that we predict will vary year by year. For example, suppose we manufacture sports goggles and sell them to retail stores. We'll want to increase our marketing efforts in years the Olympics are held. The summer games will be held in 2004, 2008, 2012, 2016, and 2020 and the winter games will be in 2006, 2010, 2014, 2018, and 2022. In years without Olympics, we budget $800 for marketing. We add $400 for summer Olympics years and $300 for Winter Olympics years. (Aren't goggles used more for winter sports? Well, yes. But people pay less attention to the Winter Olympics.) Experience indicates that the plan in Table 2-4 is a good one. We show just the first five years, but the spending pattern continues for 20 years. The $800 for year one and the $4,700 for year five show up in Table 2-2 as annual variable costs. We show the average over years in Table 2-4 to illustrate how a cyclical cost like this averages out over time. We could have just used a 20-year average and entered this as a fixed cost. But, when we know what years will be higher or lower, it's more accurate to go year by year than to use averaging.

	2003 Non-Olympic	2004 Summer Olympics	2005 Non-Olympic	2006 Winter Olympics	2007 Non-Olympic
Annual	800	1,200	800	1,100	800
Total	800	2,000	2,800	3,900	4,700
Average	800	1,000	933	975	940

Table 2-4. Annual variable costs: marketing budget for goggles based on Olympic years

Project costs. This is an example of a project that is expected to take three years, at a cost of $2,500 per year. It's happening from 2007-2009, so the first year shows up in our five-year budget, but the second and third do not show up until the 10-year budget.

Semi-variable (fixed base/variable volume). This is a single line item that is the total of multiple elements. Some of the elements do not vary per year (or with quantity of production) and others do. The total costs of any small office are like this. Fixed costs would include rent or mortgage and equipment leases. Variable costs would include supplies. Sometimes, a single line item will be semi-variable. For example, cellular telephone service has a fixed monthly cost up to a certain number of minutes per month and then a variable cost for additional use.

When you prepare a long-term budget, think about each line item in your short-term budget. Would you consider the cost to be fixed, variable, or some of each? Exactly how would you predict the cost?

Forecasting Income

Forecasting income is harder than forecasting expenses. Expenses come from decisions we make, work our team does, and things our team buys. We are in control of them (or we should be). But income is a result of choices made by our customers. If they buy from us, our income goes up. If they don't, it goes down. We can influence income through marketing and sales efforts and by producing a high-quality product that customers want, but we don't determine it. As a result, it's harder to estimate.

There are two basic approaches we can use to estimate income. We can base our forecasts on past income or on our marketing and sales plan. Let's look at each in turn.

Past Income

If we're going to make an estimate based on past income, total numbers will not tell us enough. A month-by-month breakdown will show us some useful information, but it's more important to get a picture of who is giving us money and why.

If we look at who is giving us money, we should ask these questions:

- How many current customers do we have?

- How much do they spend each month?
- How much money will we receive from committed contracts, even if we receive no new orders?
- How many new customers do we get each month?
- What is the spending pattern typical of new customers for the first year?

Using these questions, we can look at how much money has been coming in and estimate how much money is likely to be coming in later, in future months or years.

In estimating sales of current products or services to current customers, there's one other thing we should think about: How long does it take to make a sale? This is called the *sales cycle time*. It's the time from the initial contact with the customer to the purchase, including the delivery of the item. (If the purchase is on account, then the time to payment is not included.) For expensive items, salespeople might have to call on customers several times over months to close a deal. In that case, you should talk with the salespeople about how things are going now, and then predict future sales from their reports.

Smart Managing

Sales, Customer Satisfaction, and Budget Preparation

It is always good to keep in touch with our customers, and often we're looking for a reason (or even an excuse) to call them. When you're preparing your budget, you have that opportunity. For example, if a customer ordered a lot early in the year and not much recently, you can call and ask if there were any problems. You might win the customer back.

Before we finish estimating sales to current clients, we need to ask one more question: Can we sell them other products or services? Based on what they've bought in the past, what else do we

Key Term

Cycle time The length of time it takes to complete any cycle. Sales cycle time is from first contact to the client receiving the order. Production cycle time is how long it takes to get something from the beginning of the assembly line to the end.

have that they might want? Marketing people call new things to sell to old customers *vertical services.* When we want to increase sales, this is one of the best ways to do it, since it's less expensive to sell more to a current customer than to find new customers.

> **Vertical services** Products or services that we sell as additional items to existing customers. They may be add-ons or they may be separate items likely to be of interest to customers who have bought a particular item.

After that, we turn our attention to the new customers. How do we predict sales to new customers? We need to look at the marketing and sales plans and get estimates of the market. If you're not in marketing or sales, talk to people who are and get their estimates. If you are, then turn to Chapter 11, where we talk about estimating business income.

Estimating per Item Sold (Products or Services)

The second approach to estimating income is to estimate the income we expect to receive from each product or service we sell. We may find that products and services sell to different markets or at different times of year. We estimate monthly sales for each item and then add them all up to see the total income per month and for the year.

It's often a good idea to build a marketing plan for each product, service, or line that we offer. We then estimate sales

> **Bicycle Sales and Repairs**
>
> A small bike shop makes money from sales of new bikes, bike repairs, and sales of accessories. Looking at past year figures by product and by month, we see that kids' bikes and accessories have the highest sales during the Christmas shopping season, adult bikes and accessories have a small peak at Christmas and a big one in spring, and repairs peak in the spring and then continue for the summer. Because we thought about the differences between adults' and kids' bikes and accessories, we were able to make a more accurate income prediction. We were also able to improve our plan for ordering items for sale.

> **Product line** A set of related products, often with the same model name, that share a marketing plan.
>
> **Service line** A set of related services that share a marketing plan.

from the marketing plan for that particular item.

In evaluating future sales, there's a method called SWOT: Strengths, Weaknesses, Opportunities, Threats. We look at our past sales and income record and ask four questions:

- What are the strengths of our department or our product/service line that we could use to increase sales?
- What are the weaknesses of our department or our product/service line that might cause sales to fall (for example, the retirement of an experienced salesperson)? Can we do anything about those weaknesses?
- What opportunities for new sales exist? How can we take advantage of them?
- What threats, from competition, general economic problems, or anything else, exist outside our department? What can we do to respond to them effectively, to reduce the risk and cost or even to turn the threat into an opportunity?

We can revise our business strategy, our marketing plan, and our budget based on SWOT.

Expense Categories vs. Account Codes

There is one other item we may need to include in our budget. Accounting departments often assign income and expense cate-

> **Do All of SWOT**
>
> People find it easier to think about good stuff than bad stuff. We can talk about strengths and opportunities and then find an excuse to ignore weaknesses and threats. The result is unrealistic hype, not a good business plan. Focusing on the down side, on weaknesses and threats, isn't depressing; it's actually good for business. Entrepreneurs, especially, thrive on challenges. But any department benefits from a realistic assessment of weaknesses and threats—followed by a realistic plan to address them.

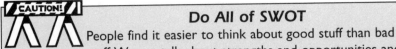

gories and account codes that they use to track budgets. If that's the case in your organization, you'll need to understand how they work so that you can use them whenever you spend money, request information from accounting, or track actual vs. estimated budgets. Table 2-5 illustrates expense codes.

			Marketing				Finance				Mfg			
			00	01	02	03	00	01	02	03	00	01	02	03
Expense Category	**Exp. Code**	**Total**	Tot											
Cost of Goods Sold	200	***$294***												
Plain paper	201	**245**	**85**	50	35		**85**	55	10	20	**75**	75		
Toner	202	**49**	**17**	10	7		**17**	11	2	4	**15**	15		
Services	300	***$150***												
Manual folding	301	**65**	**50**		50		**15**		15		**0**			
Envelope stuffing	302	**85**	**35**			35	**0**				**15**	50		

Table 2-5. Expense codes and departmental account codes

Each line item is given an expense code that is part of a series. The series number (200 and 300, in Table 2-5) shows the totals for all the items in the series. Each line item is broken out by department. Each department is allowed to have up to 99 sub-codes, 01 through 99. The total for each department is shown under the 00 code. Each number in the spreadsheet can be assigned a particular code. For example, the $35 spent by sub-account 02 within marketing for plain paper would be designated 201-MKT-02, the $50 spent by manufacturing on envelope stuffing services would be coded 302-MFG-01, and the $17 spent by finance for toner would be 202-FIN-00.

The expense code numbers for each line item allow accounting to track expenses for each line item on their computers. The groupings for department allow accounting to bill back costs for copy shop services to the various departments. And the sub-accounts let each department manage and track expenses any way the people want to. For example, in marketing they might want to separate costs for mailings from costs

> **For Example**
>
> **A Really Complicated Account Code**
>
> Account codes can get very complicated. One of my clients tracked all costs in the IT department by project, phase, and type of work. Each project had a code, from 20001 on up. For each project, phases were designated 01 through 05. There were also codes for type of work: 01 for an internal expense, 02 for contractor services, and 03 for equipment. So, if I wanted to get paid as a contractor for phase two of project 20015, then I needed to put a note on my invoice that the account code was IT-20015-02-02.

for trade shows: they use 01 for mailings, 02 for trade shows, and 03 for miscellaneous. In manufacturing they don't care what the copies are for, but want to know who requested the copies: they use 01 for the administrative assistant, 02 for the director's secretary, and 03 for the director herself.

Key Accounting Concepts

You don't need to know about accounting to make a good departmental budget, but it helps. If you know a bit about accounting, then it's easier to request information from the accounting department and to give them information and records that they need in the way they need to see them.

Accounting systems have been around since about the year 800, when the court of Emperor Charlemagne of France invented double-entry bookkeeping. So that's where we'll start.

Transactions, Double-Entry Bookkeeping, and the General Ledger

The basic unit of accounting is not money, it is the transaction. Accounting tries to record the movement of money from one place to another. The bean counters in Charlemagne's court realized that if every number was recorded twice, then it was possible to make sure that there were no errors. Every time money came from one place and went to another place, the transaction was recorded in both places. Then it became possible to balance accounts and make sure that there were no errors. This was called *double-entry bookkeeping*

Transaction A single transfer of money from one place or person to another.

Entry A record of a transaction.

Account A place to record transactions that represents a single source or use of money.

Double-entry bookkeeping A system of bookkeeping in which every transaction is recorded twice, once in the account the money is coming from and once in the account the money is going to.

Balance Compare accounts to each other to make sure that all transactions were recorded correctly.

Reconcile Compare an account with what you actually have or with an account record from another source (such as a bank or credit card company), to make sure that records are accurate and nothing is missing.

General ledger A book in which monetary transactions are copied (posted) from a journal (in the form of debits and credits). It is the final record from which financial statements are prepared. The general ledger accounts are often the control accounts that report totals of details recorded in subsidiary ledgers.

The basics of double-entry bookkeeping are easy to understand. For example, suppose you run a bakery and someone comes in and buys an éclair for a dollar. You put that dollar bill in your cash register and you record an increase of one dollar in the cash account. But where do you record the other side of the transaction? Charlemagne's accountants came up with a clever idea: they created a special category of accounts called *income accounts*. All money gets recorded there. So the dollar that came in shows up at the cash register and also in the income account. Then, at the end of the day, you check your receipts. Your total receipts, in the income account, are $500. You received $350 in cash, $100 in credit card receipts, and $50 in personal checks. Since your total income of $500 equals the total of the different categories of receipts, you know that your accounts balance and all your records are correct.

After you balance the accounts, you can reconcile them. You add up the money in your cash drawer: $375. You check your previous day's records: you had $25 in the drawer when you closed last night. Last night's closing at $25 plus the $350 from today total $375, so your cash account is reconciled with the money in the cash register.

Expense accounts work much like income accounts, except they're used to make the second transaction for money leaving the company. If we pay $20 cash for a meal at a restaurant, we reduce our cash account by $20 to match the money leaving our wallet and increase our expense account for food by $20.

The general ledger is every account with every transaction. Even accountants usually avoid working inside the general ledger. It is much easier to figure things out one or two accounts at a time.

Cash vs. Accrual

The Internal Revenue Service allows organizations to track money in one of two ways: on a *cash basis* or on an *accrual basis*. Cash basis is just what it sounds like: you count the money when the cash comes in. Accrual basis is used when we want to track the actions that generate money, even if the money isn't transferred. If you work with invoices for your customers and from your suppliers, a cash accounting system wouldn't keep track of those invoices. So, to make sure you receive from your customers and pay your suppliers, you track bills with *accounts receivable* and *accounts payable*. That way, you can keep track of money owed to the business and money the business owes others.

Account Types

In accrual accounting, we end up with all kinds of special accounts. In addition to income and expense accounts, we track accounts receivable, accounts payable, assets (the value of things owned), liabilities (the value of things owed), and inventory. We aren't going to go into all of those here—the book would be much too long. After you learn the basics of budgeting, you can take more time learning about the parts of accounting most useful to you. If you want to start now, turn to Chapter 11, Budgeting for Small Businesses, and look at the four most important standard accounting reports: the balance sheet, the income and expense statement, the cash flow statement, and the accounts receivable statement.

Right now, let's look at two reports you can get from the accounting department that can be really useful: the expense (or income and expense) statement tracking estimated vs. actual and the accounts receivable report, which will show you how quickly you are getting paid by your customers.

Tracking Expenses: Estimated vs. Actual

Table 2-6 is an estimated vs. actual budget report for March 2003 based on the budget we created for the print shop in Chapter 1. The values in the Estimated column are simply one-twelfth of the annual values you gave to the accounting department. The Actual figures are the results accounting tracked for you when you gave them usage reports, service requests, receipts, and approved payment on bills. The Variance ($) is Actual minus Estimated. The Variance (%) is calculated as the difference (Actual minus Estimated) divided by Estimated. If the percent is near zero, then what really happened was close to your estimate. If the variance is above 20% or below minus 20%, then it would be good to look at why there is a difference between estimated and actual. For example, you bought more plain paper and more toner than expected. Did you run more

Print shop expenses	March Estimated	Actual	Variance $	Variance %
Equipment leases	$200.00	200.00	$0.00	0
Toner	90.00	110.00	20.00	22
Plain paper	30.00	50.00	20.00	67
Special papers	6.00	4.00	(2.00)	–33
Equipment purchase	79.17	—	(79.17)	–100
Service contracts	133.33	133.33	0.00	0
Equipment repair	29.17	20.00	(9.17)	–31
Miscellaneous	15.00	30.00	15.00	100
Sales tax	19.95	17.12	(2.83)	–14
Total Expenses	$602.62	$564.45	$(38.17)	–6

Table 2-6. Tracking expenses: estimated vs. actual

CAUTION!

When Does a Variance Matter?

Some variances matter and others really don't. In addition, the size of the variance may matter as much as or more than the percent. For example, a variance of 33% sounds high, but it isn't a big deal that you spent $6 on specialty papers instead of $4. The 100% variance on equipment expense is not a surprise at all: you don't buy equipment every month. But if your plans change and you expect a major variance on equipment for the whole year, that is important. Does the 100% variance ($15.00) in Miscellaneous matter? It isn't much money. But it might indicate that someone on your staff is being sloppy and recording something in Miscellaneous that should be tracked in another account. Problems like that are best caught early.

Use your intelligence when analyzing variances.

copies than expected? Did you stock up because there was a big sale on supplies?

You can create a variance report that explains any significant difference between actual and estimated expenses.

Accounts Receivable and Aging

The accounts receivable aging report shows us our customers are paying us on time. Take a look at the example in Table 2-7.

This is an example of a very healthy accounts receivable aging. The age of account is the number of days past either the transaction date (the date the bill was sent) or the due date of the bill. If it is set from the due date of the bill, there will be an additional line, Currently Due, to show amounts that have been

Age of Accounts (Days)	Value of Receivables	Percent of Total Value
0 - 10	$15,000	60.0%
11 - 30	7,500	30.0%
31 - 45	2,000	8.0%
46 - 60	400	1.6%
Over 60	100	0.4%
Total Receivables	$25,000	100%

Table 2-7. Sample accounts receivable aging report

billed but are not yet overdue. In this example, the age is measured from the transaction date. Most outstanding accounts receivable are less than 10 days old and 90% are less than 30 days old. That means that you have very little to worry about in collections.

Accounting can provide detail on this report. For example, you might want a copy of the invoices for amounts due over 45 days. Perhaps you have a rule that you will not accept orders from customers with accounts 60 days past due and it's time to give some customers a friendly reminder.

The Manager's Checklist for Chapter 2

- ❑ Your budget should be based on what you're going to do, your vision, and not on last year's numbers.
- ❑ Short-term budgets, one year or less in length, are for planning and tracking.
- ❑ Long-term budgets, longer than one year, are just for planning.
- ❑ You can prepare long-term budgets by asking if expenses are fixed, variable, or partly fixed and partly variable.
- ❑ You can average expenses that vary a great deal or you can plan them more accurately.
- ❑ In estimating income, you need to think about current customers buying what they've bought before, vertical services (new items for current customers), and marketing to bring in new customers.
- ❑ You can make good estimates and also manage well using SWOT: an evaluation of strengths, weaknesses, opportunities, and threats.
- ❑ Budgeting is easier if you understand accounting basics, including account codes, transactions, and balancing and reconciling accounts.
- ❑ You need to be able to track your actual expenses against your estimates.

- ❑ You may need to work with accounts receivable aging reports to call your customers to remind them to pay their bills.

3

Gathering Production Figures

Those who cannot remember the past are condemned to repeat it.

—George Santayana

The future will not be the same as the past. We hope it will be better. But the past is a good place to start when we want to make our budget for the future. We can learn four things from the past:

- How records were organized and kept
- How much money was earned or spent at a particular time
- What trends show up in the past that may continue into the future
- What relationships there are among items in our budget

A simple example will illustrate how the relationship among line items in our budget is useful for estimation.

Suppose you want to estimate copy shop expenses for the

> **Trend** A pattern of change over time. We see it in records of the past and use it to predict or make estimates for the future.

next year. Unfortunately, you find that records were not kept well. You know that the shop spent $3,000 on paper, but toner was bought from several stores and the records weren't kept. How do you figure out how much toner you'll need this year?

Going back to earlier years, you find that when the copy shop spent $3,000 on paper, it spent $750 on toner and when it spent $2,000 on paper, it spent $500 on toner. You see the relationship: for every $1,000 the copy shop spends on paper, it spends $250 on toner. For this year, you can estimate that the toner expense will be 25% of the paper expense. Logically, this relationship makes sense because the amount of paper used and the amount of toner used are both results of the number of copies made.

Gathering Past Figures

There are three sources of past figures: actual numbers from the past, prior estimates, and past tax returns. The actual figures are definitely the best choice, because they tell us what really happened. If they are not available, we should look at estimates and tax returns. Estimates, of course, might have

> **Numbers Don't Create Numbers**
>
> When working with trends and relationships, it's important to remember that we're not saying that past numbers cause future numbers or that one number causes another. Management decisions and business actions determine the numbers. The patterns in the numbers, such as trends, are results, not causes.
>
> For example, we can determine that the relationship between paper expenses and toner expenses is a ratio of 4:1, but if the price of paper goes up, then that ratio would change, so our estimate would have to change. Be sure you understand what's actually happening in the business that creates trends and relationships.

been wrong; without the actual figures, we have no way of knowing. Tax returns are a good source in one way: we can always get them, since corporate accounting will have a copy. However, the figures presented on tax returns are quite a bit different from the numbers we use to manage our department internally during the year. This is not tax cheating, but the result of legitimate alternatives for presenting information to the Internal Revenue Service (IRS).

Using Actual Figures

You can get actual figures for previous accounting periods from the accounting system if books were properly kept in the last accounting period. It's good to look at several periods if you can get them. You should request the figures in a format that's easy for you. If you're going to prepare a monthly budget, you should get monthly figures, and so forth. Also, it's much easier to use figures in a spreadsheet program than printed reports. There are very few things more irritating than typing numbers into a computer when they came from a computer but were provided in hard copy.

The accounting department is not the only source of past figures. Some departments keep internal records. Sometimes, we can't find any internal records at all, but we can request a copy of our account from a vendor or credit card company. Of course, this information may be incomplete. Any figures we can get fairly easily are worth it. However, at a certain point, we don't want to waste time gathering past numbers and spending hours organizing a past budget. There are other ways of figuring out our budget for this year.

Ask for Help — TRICKS OF THE TRADE

This may sound simple, but never hesitate to ask for help from the folks in accounting when you get your figures. Account codes, in particular, can be confusing. Most accountants understand that, as specialists, part of their job is to explain accounting to other managers. If you've had a bad experience, where you were criticized for asking or you got an answer that made no sense, find someone else and try again.

Smart Managing

Closing the Gap

We may run into two gaps when we gather past figures. First, some figures may be missing. Second, two sources may disagree. Maybe accounting says we spent a certain amount on supplies and our records show a different number. When we find these gaps, we should try to understand the reasons. If we can get detailed line items to compare, that makes it much easier because we can drill down and find the differences.

When numbers are simply missing, we may be able to do some calculations. We might have a total figure for the budget (possibly on the corporate financial statement or tax returns), so we can subtract the figures we do have for some categories and what remains is the amount of money spent on the unknown categories.

Once we have our past figures, we should lay them out in a spreadsheet and create a new column (or columns) for our new estimates, as we did in Chapter 1.

Using Estimated Figures

If we can't find actual figures, and even if we can, it's good to have the estimates for the prior months or years. If we don't have past actual figures, then this is likely to be the best we can get. And if we do have past actual figures, then the estimates can still be useful in two ways.

First, we can set up a very convenient spreadsheet that shows past estimated figures and past actual figures, then add a new column for our estimates for the next period.

Second, we may find that there are budgetary assumptions that we or the previous manager wrote. We can use those assumptions or adjust them based on what we've learned since they were made. Sometimes, the budgetary assumptions may tell us where to find the missing actual figures.

If all we have are estimates, then we should think about setting them aside and starting from scratch. Remember, we have no way of knowing if the estimates reflect what was actually earned or spent in the past period.

Using Tax Returns

Past tax records will be the most accurate source for at least one item: payroll. The IRS keeps close track of both salaried (W-2) and contract (1099) workers and the payroll figures for tax deposits. (We discuss this further in Chapter 10.)

There's one exception to this rule. Certain industries, such as restaurants and delivery services, allow tips from customers and may also receive cash and use it to pay staff without recording it. The IRS has rules for these companies and many companies follow the rules. Those that don't may be following old customs, but they're breaking the law and taking a big risk. As our society becomes more computerized, the IRS finds these transactions easier and easier to track. It is best if our internal accounts, our actual income, and our payroll pay rates match both what we really do and what we report to the IRS.

Working with Multiple Periods

When we've gathered all the past numbers, we need to put them together and make sense of them. In doing this, we need to pay attention to the organization of the past periods that we're using. There are two parts to this. The first is that the records may be a mix of daily, weekly, monthly, quarterly, semi-annual, or annual, and we need to bring these together. Second, if we have records from multiple past periods, we have to know how to use all of them for putting together our new estimates.

Converting Time Periods

We need to adjust our information into the best time periods for our budget. We should always make our estimates for each item in the time period that is easiest, as it will be most accurate. But then we need to adjust so that everything fits together. For example, some companies pay clerical staff every two weeks and professional staff once a month. If so, we should make our payroll estimate for clerical staff by the week and our estimate for professional staff by the month. We can use the calculator in Table 3-1 to adjust the differences.

	Daily	Weekly	Monthly	Annual
Daily	$ ENTER	Annual/52	Annual/12	Daily x 250
Weekly	Annual/250	$ ENTER	Annual/12	Weekly x 52
Monthly	Annual/250	Annual/52	$ ENTER	Monthly x 12
Annual	Annual/250	Annual/52	Annual/12	$ ENTER

Table 3-1. Converter for estimation period (formulas)

Table 3-1 shows how pay for any one period is calculated for the other three periods, so you can make one in your own spreadsheet program. In each row, one cell is left blank for you to enter the number to calculate across periods. That number is then annualized, that is, multiplied by the appropriate figure to determine pay per year. Then the annual figure is divided by the appropriate number to give the daily, weekly, and monthly figures.

	Daily	Weekly	Monthly	Annual
Daily	$15.00	$72.12	$312.50	$3,750.00
Weekly	$20.80	$100.00	$433.33	$5,200.00
Monthly	$38.40	$184.62	$800.00	$9,600.00
Annual	$48.00	$230.77	$1,000.00	$12,000.00

Table 3-2. Converter for estimation period (example)

Table 3-2 shows sample calculations. For example, $100 a week is $433.33 per month, not $400—which is what we would calculate if we figured a month as four weeks—and $800 per month is only $184.62 per week, not $200.00.

The daily figure used here is based on 250 days per year. This would be accurate for a company with a five-day work week that closes 10 days a year for holidays. The number that you should use will vary depending on the company calendar. And, if you're calculating costs per employee, you need to decide if you want to measure those costs per active workday or

There Are Not Four Weeks in a Month

A very common estimating mistake is to think quickly, "There are four weeks in a month, so something that costs $200 a week means $800 a month." Four weeks is 28 days, but only February has just 28 days (usually); four have 30 and seven have 31. If we estimate based on four weeks a month, we may run out of cash unexpectedly in long months. This is especially a problem for businesses that run slow in the summer, where July and August are two long months in a row. And the line items we calculate this way will be low by about 8% for the year.

per paid workday, as we discussed in Chapter 2. An employee typically has about 222 active workdays after vacation days, holidays, sick days, and personal leave days are taken out. But a regular five-day-a-week employee is paid for 260 days per year.

What Is Your Work Week?

If our store makes an average of $5,000 per day, how much does it make in a week? That may sound like a simple question, but it isn't. Our store is likely to be open six days a week or maybe seven. But maybe we're in a business district and we're open just five days a week. When I was growing up in Philadelphia, there was a restaurant called Thursday Too, which was open three days a week.

We need to adjust our budgets for days of the week and hours each day. How much this matters depends on our business. For storefronts open to the public, especially, it can be crucial.

Any business that has sales has to adjust its monthly income expectations based on the number of work days in the month, as well as seasonal factors. You may also have to budget for extra help during the busy season or save money by cutting to a four-day workweek during slack time. In making these adjustments, you have to pay attention to available cash and the amount of business. This is especially true for companies that need to prepare for busy seasons: there may be much work to be done—and paid for—before the money comes in.

Smart Managing

Get to Know Your Business Better

One manager of a small health food and vitamin store felt that he was wasting his time and the company's money by staying open until 10:00 every night instead of closing at 9:00. But he didn't just decide to change the closing hour. He tallied the register at 9:00 every night for two months. When he closed at 10:00, he checked the difference to find out how much money the store made in the last hour. After two months he saw that, though sales were sporadic, they paid off. He kept the late hours and made more money.

The smart manager experiments and goes with what works, rather than making decisions based on assumptions without evidence.

Budgeting for Multiple-Shift Operations

So far, we've been discussing only companies that run one shift per day. If we work at a store that has long hours or a factory that runs all the time, we need to be able to create budgets for multiple shifts. Let's pick a simple example: a manufacturing facility that runs 24/7, that is, 24 hours a day, 7 days a week, but shuts down one week a year for facilities maintenance. Staff attend training during their week off. Tables 3-3 and 3-4 show a spreadsheet that lets you calculate costs for any time period and see what they are for any other time period.

If we enter a cost or an income item in the shaded cell on any line, the spreadsheet will calculate that cost or income for all other time periods. The first six columns are for items that apply 52 weeks per year, such as rent. The second set of six columns shows results per the work year, which is 51 weeks. For example, if electricity costs $100 per hour for the 51 weeks the plant is operating, that is only $98 per hour divided over the 52-week year. On the other hand, if a piece of equipment rents for $100 per week, and we pay the rental fee all year, although it's used only 51 weeks a year, then it should be worth $102 per week of operation.

If you want to create a similar spreadsheet, the formulas are shown in Table 3-4. We have included only one line of formulas and split it into two rows so that it will fit on the page. You

	Calendar Year (52 weeks)					
	Hour	Shift	Day	Week	Month	Year
If hourly	100	800	2400	16846	73000	876000
If per shift	13	100	300	2106	9125	109500
If daily	4	33	100	702	3042	36500
If weekly	0.59	4.75	14.25	100	433	5200
If monthly	0.14	1.10	3.29	23	100	1200
If annual	0.01	0.09	0.27	2	8	100
If hourly	98	785	2354	16523	71600	859200
If per shift	12	98	294	2065	8950	107400
If daily	4	33	98	688	2983	35800
If weekly	0.58	4.66	13.97	98	425	5100
If monthly	0.13	1.07	3.22	23	98	1177
If annual	0.01	0.09	0.27	2	8	100

	Production Year (51 weeks)					
	Hour	Shift	Day	Week	Month	Year
If hourly	102	816	2447	17176	73000	876000
If per shift	13	102	306	2147	9125	109500
If daily	4	34	102	716	3042	36500
If weekly	0.61	4.84	14.53	102	433	5200
If monthly	0.14	1.12	3.35	24	100	1200
If annual	0.01	0.09	0.28	2	8	100
If hourly	100	800	2400	16847	71600	859200
If per shift	13	100	300	2106	8950	107400
If daily	4	33	100	702	2983	35800
If weekly	0.59	4.75	14.25	100	425	5100
If monthly	0.14	1.10	3.29	23	100	1177
If annual	0.01	0.09	0.28	2	8	100

Table 3-3. Converter for estimation periods with hours and shifts (example)

should be able to build the full spreadsheet from this example.

When building spreadsheets like this one, it's important to understand them clearly and to make any adjustments you need. For example, in Table 3-3, the monthly column works for 11 months of the year, but you would need a special spreadsheet for the month when the annual downtime occurs.

Hour 1	Shft 1	Day 1	Week 1	Month 1	Year 1
100	Year1/(365*3)	Year1*365	Year 1/52	Year1/12	Hour*265*3*8
Hour 2	**Shft 2**	**Day 2**	**Week 2**	**Month 2**	**Year 2**
Year2/(358*3*8)	Year 2/(365*3)	Year2/358	Year2/51	Year2/12	=Year1

Table 3-4. Converter for estimation periods with hours and shifts (formulas)

Working with Account Categories and Line Item Names

The production figures from past years or months will probably be in the standard income and expense format we introduced in Chapters 1 and 2, with line items and amounts. If they are not, you should set up a spreadsheet and enter them. However, you should not assume that last year's categories are right for this year. You may find that certain line items are not needed any more and you may find that you need some new line items. Also, you might decide that you want to split items or combine items. Set up the line items for this year's budget in the way that makes sense for this year.

Evaluating the Quality of Your Information

We want to base our new estimates on good past information. How do we know that the information we have is accurate?

If past records come from the accounting department, we can trust that they are probably as good as we'll get. If you can speak to the accountant or bookkeeper who worked on the files last year, he or she can tell you if there were any adjusting

Check Categories Before Creating Estimates

Whether or not you change line item categories, you should check your list of categories (and account codes, if your company uses them) with the accounting department before you get too far on your budget. It is easier to get all of the categories and account codes correct and approved, and then work on your estimates. If you do the estimates, and then need to change your categories, it takes a lot of extra work and it's easy to make errors.

entries that might point to poor record keeping. If there were none, trust the figures you have. If there were any, ask the accountant to let you know which line items had errors and help you decide on the best figure to use for future estimation.

Adjusting entry An entry made by an accountant to fix errors, make up for lost information, or adjust internal books to match the books filed with tax forms.

On the other hand, if you were digging receipts out of old shoeboxes, then you have less reason to trust last year's figures. Here are some things you can do:

- Assume that bank records, cancelled checks, and vendor records marked "paid" were verified by someone who probably kept good records. They are more trustworthy.
- Contact vendors and banks and ask for records of any business with your department for the past time period.
- Sort your sources and decide which ones are more reliable. If there were good records in some months and not others, then use the months that had good records to make a good guess at the other figures.
- Use common sense. For example, if you're managing a Christmas gift shop and you're missing last year's figures for November, don't use August figures for November. Use an average of the last week in October and the first week of December for each week in November.

When you have the best figures you can get and when you know how good you think they are, you're ready to start working on this year's estimate. However, don't assume that the future will be like the past. Ask yourself how the department has changed from last year to this year. Here are some important questions:

- Does the department have the same customers?
- Is it doing the same work it did in other years and offering the same products and services?
- What external changes, such as good or bad years in the economy or your industry, will have an effect?
- Has the department changed the way it does business? Is staff reorganized? Is the number of people the same?
- Are there vacancies you will fill this year?
- Do you expect to hire new people?
- Have you made any recent efforts to reduce costs or increase sales that might make a difference in the upcoming months or year?

Working with Multiple Periods and Trends

The more information we have about the past, the better we can estimate the future budget for our department. But we have to know how to use that information in a smart way.

Comparing Line Items

Look at all the prior periods. Do they have the same line items? If not, when new ones were added, might the new line items have been created by splitting prior period categories? For example, if we see that the most recent year has two lines, "office equipment" and "office supplies," but the preceding year has "general office" and all the other lines are the same, it's a pretty good guess that the two new lines were split from "general office." If you suspect that the categories are different from period to period, do not use those line items for trend analysis.

Thinking About Ranges

Income and costs go up and down. If you have two or more past periods to look at, you should figure that the next period will be between the highest and lowest past periods, unless you have a good reason to think otherwise. We can think of the lowest past figure as our minimum estimate, the highest as the maximum, and the difference between them as the range of variation.

Thinking About Trends

If you have several past periods, you can look for trends. For example, you might see that a line item has gone up almost every quarter for the past two years. It would be a good first guess to think that it will keep going up and at about the same rate. However, you should test this thinking before you finish estimating. Why are costs going up? Are you buying more of something? Is the price per item increasing? Why is income going up? Do you have more new customers? Are your old customers buying more? Are you raising your prices? Get a sense of what is happening and make your estimates based on business processes and actual costs and transactions; don't base future numbers simply on past numbers.

Trends don't only go up or down. For example, if you looked at a history of 10 years of expenses for the sports goggle marketing shown in Figure 2-4, you would see an up-and-down cycle every four years. But you would know it was tied to the Olympics only if someone told you the reason behind the spending decisions.

Manager's Checklist for Chapter 3

- ❑ Numbers don't create numbers; they report business decisions, conditions, and actions—facts that you can study to generate numbers.
- ❑ Analyzing relationships and trends can help you make future estimates.

- ❑ You can get past figures from actual results, estimates, and tax returns.
- ❑ When making estimates, there's often a natural time period for your estimate. Use that time period, and then use a converter for estimation periods spreadsheet calculator to calculate for other time periods.
- ❑ When creating a converter for estimation periods spreadsheet calculator, be sure you follow the calendar of your department for hours, shifts, days, weeks, and months.
- ❑ Remember that you sometimes want to adjust costs for different ways of counting time, as when you want to distribute an employee's total salary across his or her productive work hours.
- ❑ Past actual results are the best basis for estimates; you can get them from accounting or by putting together statements from vendors and customers with the best records you can find.
- ❑ Evaluate the quality of records before you use them for estimating.
- ❑ You should understand past budget categories, but be free to consider new ones that make more sense for the way the department works.
- ❑ Verify account categories, line item names, and account codes with the accounting department before you prepare your new estimates.

4

Creating a Production Budget

The great cycle of the ages is renewed.

—Virgil

This chapter will help you build a budget for production work, that is, for ongoing business operations. Each year, the cycle of business repeats, but with changes. The challenge of budgeting for a department is to figure out what will change and what will stay the same. With past figures in hand, we're ready to put together our best estimate of what the next year (or months) will look like. Some of the methods also apply to long-term budgets; we'll note which methods are suitable. We will discuss:

- Methods for estimating income and expenses
- How to put your budget together, step by step
- A sample budget for a production group or manufacturing environment

Estimation Methods

There's a fundamental difference between how we estimate income and how we estimate expenses.

Our income is the result of the decisions our customers make and the actions they take. (Do they buy what we sell? Do they buy from us? How quickly do they pay their bills?) We can influence income by making a good product or service, marketing it well, selling it well, and maintaining good customer support and customer relations. But the decision is not ours. An income estimate is a guess about how much we'll make based on what other people will do.

Expenses are different. Departmental expenses are the result of decisions that we make within our department. The real question isn't "How much will we spend?" The real questions are "What do we want to do? What will it cost to do what we want to do? How will we spend our money? What is the total?" For expenses, we do need to think about what will happen, but what really matters is what we are going to do.

Thinking About What Will Change

If everything were going to stay exactly the same and we were going to do everything the same this year as we did last year, we would just copy last year's actual figures for this year's budget and we'd be done. The art of budgeting is in deciding what we think will change and what we think will stay the same. We should think about changes in this order: changes outside our control first, and then what we will do differently.

Changes Outside Our Control

If people are buying more (or less) of what we sell, we will need to buy more (or fewer) components and pay for more (or less) labor. If we're buying the same amount of something, but the price per item is going up or down, then we'll need to adjust our budget accordingly. When we think about changes outside our control, we should review each line item: first income items, then expense items.

For each income item, ask the following questions, in this order:

1. What changes do we expect in quantity purchased from current customers? What changes do we expect in quantity purchased from new customers? (See "Planning the Future in Detail," below, for ways to answer these questions.)
2. Are there changes in our company's prices for existing items? We adjust our prices for these changes. (If you set prices yourself, see Chapter 11 for some tips.)
3. Are we selling any new products or services? Using the marketing plan, we estimate income from these new products or services.
4. Are we selling to any new markets? Using the marketing plan, we estimate income from these new markets.

Along with the income figures, we'll have our production plan. Our production plan is crucial in guiding our expense budget. You will see why later in this chapter, when we look at a sample manufacturing budget.

Percentage Increases and Decreases

Some businesses estimate changes in line item values by applying the same percentage-rate increase to several items. There are reasons for doing this—some of them good, some of them bad.

Sometimes, a company needs to cut expenses and the financial office just tells all departments to cut every item by, say, 10%. If you have a block budget, you can re-arrange your budget, as long as you stay within the total spending limit. If you have a line-item budget, you might have to negotiate changes to keep one line item higher by reducing others more than 10%.

Sometimes, a company responds to general economic indicators such as the cost of living or market indicators such as an industry-wide increase in prices, by adjusting line items in percentages. This only accounts for an expected change in price, but two further adjustments may be required. First of all, you need to make sure that the general changes apply to these specific items from your vendors and see if you can cut a better deal. Second, you need to consider if you'll change the quantity of an item that you're buying.

Some percentage increases are the result of contracts or policies, such as annual raises, or the results of a specific vendor announcing a price increase. These are good to use, but you should be sure that no other changes, such as a change in staffing levels, will alter the line item.

Some items, such as sales tax and interest payments, are calculated as percentages. If these rates change, adjust the appropriate line items in your budget to match.

Some managers use percentage increases as a quick way to create an estimate. We don't recommend this, because this is getting numbers from numbers, not from reality.

> Smart Managing
>
> **Making Sense of Percents**
>
> The smart manager uses percentage changes, but always checks two things for each line item:
>
> - Does the percentage change apply to this line item?
> - Are there any other changes that would also change this line item?
>
> The smart manager does not use percentage increases across line items as a quick way of making an estimate.

Planning the Future in Detail

Let's take a closer look at the methods for estimating line items that we used in Chapter 1. Start with the largest item on your estimation form and work down until only small ones are left. For each one, decide which method or methods to use in planning the budget for that line item. Here is a list of methods in the order it's best to follow:

1. Think about how your department will work this year and make a list of any changes. Then ask if each change will affect each line item and adjust those items that will change.
2. Consider purchases and leases. If you pay for an item on a contract, you should determine if those contracts continue

through the next period and what the prices will be. You should also negotiate any new contracts or at least confirm expectations of price changes with your vendors. This approach is best for fixed costs; it also works for variable costs if you know how much you'll be producing this year.

3. Talk to people. Find out what current customers plan to do; lock in contracts if you can. Do the same with vendors. Then, ask the members of your team how they want to do their work this year. Then, plan for what they'll need to spend to do it. If you don't have good records from prior years, talk to your team about how you'll keep better records through the year this time.
4. Estimate variable costs based on production. See the example later in this chapter for details.
5. By this point, you should have finished most of the major items. If any individual items worth over 10% of the total are still not finished, tackle those next.
6. Review the whole budget to make sure it makes sense.
7. Look at last year's total value for the items you haven't estimated yet and calculate the percent of last year's actual budget they represent. If that percentage is small, decide how much time you want to spend on those items.
8. For the remaining items, work on the ones most likely to change a lot first. Use any of the above methods or, if appropriate, the ones below.
9. Determine if an item can be calculated from another item. If the calculation is precise, such as sales tax, go ahead and do it. If the calculation is approximate, such as estimating the total cost of toner from the cost of paper, do it, but check your assumptions more closely.
10. Check your figures. Then have someone else check them, too.
11. Add budgetary assumptions.

As you work on each line in the budget, you may find that you can't calculate the item using just one method. Perhaps you're looking at equipment leasing and see that you have current leases and also have plans to get a lot of new equipment. Or perhaps you're looking at office supplies and it's easy to estimate the amount of money spent for the regular coffee, but you don't have good records for parties and open houses where your customers meet the staff, because people spent cash and got reimbursed.

If something like that happens, split the item. For the leasing, calculate current lease costs, then go to Chapter 5 and create a project budget for getting new equipment. For the open houses and parties, create a marketing plan and build a budget for it. If your company uses account codes, you can use subcodes to track these separate items and the accounting system will generate the totals for you, for both the estimates now and the actual figures during the year. See Chapter 2 for details on account codes and Chapter 9 for budgetary tracking. In Chapter 7, we'll show you how to combine different parts of your budget into one spreadsheet.

Also, don't hesitate to create new line items or divide line items into sub-items if that helps you make a better estimate. If accounting doesn't want you to make too many changes to line

For Example

Sometimes, Names Matter

Sometimes, the names of line items matter. For example, two line items you will often see on expense budgets are "publications and subscriptions" and "dues and memberships." Running a small business, I often join associations and get free newsletters or magazines with the membership. When I was inexperienced, I worried about which category to use. Then I got bothered, because items would go into one category or another and I really couldn't keep track of things. Then I spoke to my accountant. I learned that if an expense could go into either category, it was better to put it into "publications and subscriptions." It turns out that the IRS requires that companies put country-club memberships into "dues and memberships," and then watches the category closely to see if the company is spending too much on executive perks that should be counted as salary. I don't belong to a country club, so I moved everything into "publications and subscriptions" at the beginning of the new year.

items, you can still create your own sub-items for the estimates and then total them when you give the results to accounting.

A Sample Manufacturing Budget

Creating a manufacturing budget is a highly structured process. We get good results by going through an orderly, step-by-step process, turning our work plan into a budget. The example in this section is much simpler than we would find in the real world, but the principles and practices would apply to more complex situations.

In our example, the company purchases components (central processing units [CPUs], keyboards, and monitors), assembles the computer systems, and ships them for sale. We have no variations in the product and only one product in the line. However, we could apply this example to each product we manufacture and combine the results to build our budget.

How Much Will We Produce?

For each product model, we need to ask how many items we'll produce in the coming year. Manufacturing plants are expensive, so, in general, we want to make as many as we can, so we're manufacturing at the plant's capacity. However, we also want to ask if we can sell all that we produce or if we could sell even more than we can produce. When considering sales volume in comparison with production volume, we have several choices:

- If we can sell just about as many as we can produce, then we don't change what we're doing.
- If sales could be considerably higher than capacity, we might want to increase capacity. We could either expand our plant with another assembly line or open another plant. If we do, we should prepare a production budget for what we'll manufacture with existing assembly lines, a project budget for the changes we are making, and a separate production budget for items made on new

assembly lines. When we add them all together, we'll have the departmental budget. (Budgeting a project is discussed in Chapter 5. Putting together parts of a budget is covered in Chapter 7.)

- If sales are considerably lower than what we can produce, we have several options. We can cut production and make money with the excess plant capacity some other way. We might make another product. We might lease the space and equipment to another company. We could also manufacture at capacity and cut our prices to sell more or plan to reduce prices later in the year to reduce excess inventory.
- If we're making multiple products and selling more of some than we can make but less of others than we're making, we can convert our assembly lines to produce more of what will sell and less of what won't. This is called changing the product mix.

Table 4-1 shows a budget for expected sales and units to be produced. We aren't measuring dollars here; we're measuring the number of computers we'll assemble. It's October. The marketing department has told us that the company will be able to sell 50,000 computers next year and they want to know if we can make enough and how much it will cost to make them. Let's show them what we know!

First, we go back and ask them how many units they expect

Expected sales (number of computers)	50,000
Add: desired ending inventory of finished goods	10,000
Total Needs	60,000
Less: beginning inventory of finished goods	5,000
Units to be produced	55,000

Figure 4-1. Expected sales and units to be produced

to sell in January of the following year. We want to make sure we have an ending inventory enough to support sales for that additional month. We remember that, at the beginning of this year, there weren't enough computers to go out the door in January and we don't want that to happen again. They tell us they expect to sell 10,000 units the January after next, so we plug that in as our desired ending inventory of finished goods.

Next, we go to the production manager and ask her how many computers will be left in our warehouse at the end of this year. She tells us there will be 5,000. That's our ending inventory for this year, which is also our beginning inventory of finished goods for next year.

We put all of this together in Table 4-1 and we see that we want to produce 55,000 computers.

Inventory Management

Before we go on to calculate the cost of producing 55,000 computers, let's take a brief look at inventory management. This is only the briefest introduction to the topic. Inventory management includes counting and accounting for items we have in storage. The items can be parts to be assembled, raw materials, partially assembled components, or finished goods.

Inventory is the quantity of items we have on hand. We always have two figures, the number in our accounting books (*book* inventory) and the actual number in the warehouse (*physical* inventory). To ensure accuracy in our accounting, we take inventory: we count the items in the warehouse. Taking inventory is time-consuming and costly, so we try to keep our accounts accurate by tracking the items that come into the warehouse and the items that go out. Taking inventory may reveal a discrepancy due to accounting errors, poor tracking of items, or theft. We need to adjust our books and explain the discrepancy.

Key Term

Direct materials Parts and components that go into our finished goods. Direct materials are variable cost items, because they vary according to how much we produce.

Book inventory Materi-als, parts, supplies, and goods on hand at a given time according to records maintained for routine business activities.

Physical inventory Materials, parts, supplies, and goods on hand at a given time according to an actual count of the items.

Book value The dollar value of an item (such as an inventory item) as recorded for accounting purposes. This may be different from the value of an item if it were sold, which is called the *market value*.

There are three basic approaches to inventory, which we remember by their acronyms: FIFO, LIFO, and JIT. Imagine a shelf where we stock items. We'll put one item in each spot on the shelf and then put the next one in front of it.

- **With first in, first out (FIFO)**, we have a shelf with two sides. We put new items on the shelf from one side and the people who need them take them off from the other side. The first item we put in is the first one they take out. FIFO is best for items that have a short shelf life, because items on the shelf the longest go out first.
- **In last in, first out (LIFO)**, the shelf has only one side. We add items, pushing older ones back. When people want to take items away, they take from the front of the shelf, leaving older items in back.
- **In just-in-time (JIT) delivery**, the company tries to time production so it produces and/or delivers items just as they're needed and to time delivery of materials and supplies so it has what it needs just as it needs them.

The choice of FIFO, LIFO, or JIT matters, both for accounting of the dollar value of inventory and also for maintaining the physical inventory for production. In accounting, the costs of parts and labor change, and the book value of each item in inventory depends on those costs. If we're using FIFO, the oldest items leave the physcial inventory and are sent to customers first. As a result, all the items in inventory are made more recently than if we were using LIFO. Therefore, the cost of goods for a particular quantity of items in physical inventory will be different. If prices are going up, then a FIFO inventory value of a particular quantity of a certain physical item will cost more than a LIFO inventory of the same quantity of the same item because the parts and labor come from a later date. With JIT, inventory is minimized, so inventory costs may be less, but there may be costs for managing the flow from suppliers and to customers.

LIFO, FIFO, and JIT matter to our manufacturing plan for a number of reasons. We'll mention just two of these reasons.

When we assemble the computers, we have to test the compatibility of the components. Sometimes, our suppliers send a new keyboard that won't work with the old CPU. We'll have less trouble if we use FIFO, because each computer is more likely to be made of parts purchased at the same time. If we use LIFO, we could end up stuck with a bunch of old parts that don't work with a new version of another component.

JIT takes a lot of careful management and very reliable suppliers. If we miscalculate our needs or our suppliers slip up, we might have to hold up production waiting for parts or raw materials. If we miscalculate our production or delivery or a problem arises, we might not provide products when our customers expect them.

Calculating the Direct Materials Budget

Once we know how much we'll produce, we need to calculate how many of each part and how much of each raw material we need to buy and how much each will cost. Table 4-2, the direct materials budget, illustrates how we calculate these items.

On the top line, we enter the quantity of a given part we'll need for each finished item. In our simple example, we need one CPU, one monitor, and one keyboard for each computer.

The next three lines of this table are taken from Table 4-1, except that we multiply by the figure in "materials needed per unit." Then, for each item, we subtract the inventory we expect to have on hand at the beginning of the year. (This is a parts

JIT Jitters

This story is embarrassing, so I won't name the company where it happened. A major TV manufacturer built a plant to produce TV tubes. They put the TV tube plant right across the street from the TV manufacturing plant to save shipping costs. The TV tube plant started with sand and produced finished TV tubes. To reduce costs further, they planned to use JIT and had very little warehouse space.

Due to computer system and management problems, they did a poor job managing inventory. They made too many TV tubes and had to rent a warehouse half a mile away to store them. Now, every TV tube had to be moved half a mile to storage and then half a mile back to the plant across the street.

To make it worse, it seems they couldn't keep track of their product. While I was doing a training class at the plant, someone ran in to deliver the bad news that they'd just found another 10,000 TV tubes in the warehouse. (Having extra inventory is bad in JIT; you're paying for storage space and doing a poor job scheduling production.)

inventory, which is different from the inventory of finished goods used in Table 4-1.)

Why do we repeat three rows from Table 4-1? In this simple example, we didn't need to. But if we set up an assembly line in several stages, then we might need those extra lines. Suppose that we assemble CPUs from components, instead of buying them. We might end the year with 5,000 assembled CPUs in inventory. Since these are not finished goods (fully assembled computers), we call them our "in-progress inventory." We would place them on the "in-progress inventory" line and subtract them from the total we need to produce.

The result is the "direct materials to be purchased" line, which that tells us how many of each item we need to order. Once we know that quantity, we're ready to negotiate with our suppliers. When we negotiate, we have two goals: to keep the price as low as possible and to try to get a commitment for as long as possible that the price won't go up. In our budgetary assumptions, we should note if these per-unit costs are based on committed contracts, estimates, or a combination of the two.

	CPU	Monitor	Keyboard
Materials needed per unit	1	1	1
Total production needs (units times production needs)	55,000	55,000	55,000
Less in-progress inventory	0	0	0
Add: desired ending inventory	10,000	10,000	10,000
Total direct materials needed	65,000	65,000	65,000
Less: beginning inventory materials	2,000	3,000	1,500
Direct materials to be purchased	63,000	62,000	63,500
Cost per unit	$300	$100	$25
Cost of materials (per item)	$18,900,000	$6,200,000	$1,587,500
Sum of materials to be purchased (all items)			**$26,687,500**

Table 4-2. Direct materials budget

We finish the direct materials budget by multiplying the number of units we plan to buy for each component times the cost per unit. Then we add all of these to determine the total cost of materials to be purchased for all items (parts and raw materials).

Calculating Direct Labor Costs

We calculate the total hours of direct labor, as shown in Table 4-3, by multiplying the time it takes to assemble each unit by the number of units we're producing. How do we know how long it will take? If we haven't done this already, we should build the estimates by finding out how long each task takes on each assembly line. Alternatively, we can count the units produced in a given number of hours while a given number of people are working. However, the more detail we have, the better we'll be able to make our estimates and the better we'll be able to predict the results of change and manage our staff.

We calculate direct labor costs by multiplying the hours each employee works by the cost of paying that employee. The

Units to be produced	55,000
Labor time per unit (hours)	1.25
Total direct labor budget (hours)	68,750
Direct labor costs per hour	$15.00
Total direct labor cost	$1,031,250

Table 4-3. Direct labor costs

actual cost per hour of our staff is greater than the hourly pay rate. We must allow for Social Security, medical, and other benefits. If the staff budget is under your control or if you want to know more about expenses for human resources, turn to Chapter 10. You also need to consider the difference between the time spent in actual production and the time you pay them for, including non-production activities, vacations, and holidays, as discussed in Chapter 3.

Key Term

Direct labor Labor used directly in the production of finished goods, which is counted in the cost of goods sold. Direct labor is calculated as a variable cost of manufacturing: the more we produce, the more labor we need.

Indirect labor Labor that is not directly tied to manufacturing costs, such as supervisors and administrative staff. It may be counted in the cost of goods sold or it may be an expense item.

Calculating Overhead

Not all costs of production are directly tied to each item produced. Some items are part of your cost of operations—overhead. Costs that are the same whatever the quantity of finished goods you produce are *fixed* overhead. Costs that vary with the quantity of finished goods you produce are *variable* overhead. This includes the cost of packing materials and of receiving, shipping, and storing parts. Table 4-4 shows how to account for overhead in your budget.

Variable overhead	
Indirect materials	$15,000
Materials handling	$7,500
Fixed overhead	
Indirect labor (supervisors)	$10,000
Maintenance	$3,600
Rent	$6,000
Depreciation	$1,500
Utilities	$5,000
Total manufacturing overhead	$48,600

Table 4-4. Estimate of overhead

We estimate our fixed overhead costs by looking at past actual figures and seeing what will change, as we discussed earlier in this chapter.

Completing the Cost of Goods Sold Budget

We can now assemble our budget and calculate the total cost of goods sold, as shown in Table 4-5. The work-in-progress items would be used if we had items that were partway through production at the beginning or end of the year. We also see a zero for our end-of-year parts inventory; we plan to end the year with all parts assembled into finished goods. In our simple example, we are assuming that the price of parts hasn't changed from last year to this year.

Overhead The costs of operating a business that are not direct costs of production. Overhead is counted as part of the cost of goods sold.

Fixed overhead Overhead that will cost the same regardless of the quantity of finished goods produced.

Variable overhead Overhead that varies with the quantity of finished goods produced.

Indirect materials Items purchased by a manufacturing operation that are not included in the actual items being produced. An example would be packing materials.

When you do your budget, have the accounting department help you with LIFO, FIFO, or JIT inventory value calculations.

Beginning work-in-progress	—		
Manufacturing Costs			
Direct materials:			
Beginning inventory	$937,500		
Purchases	$26,687,500		
Materials available for manufacturing	$27,625,000		
Less: Ending parts inventory			
Total direct materials costs		$27,625,000	
Direct labor		$1,031,250	
Manufacturing overhead			
Total manufacturing costs		$48,600	$28,704,850
Less: Ending work-in-progress			—
Cost of goods manufactured			$28,704,850
Add: Beginning finished goods inventory			$2,125,000
Less: Ending finished goods inventory			$4,250,000
Cost of goods sold			$26,579,850

Table 4-5. Cost of goods sold budget

The items listed in the first column of numbers show the figures for direct materials. In the second column, we add direct labor and manufacturing overhead to get our total manufacturing costs. In the third column, we then make three adjustments to this figure based on the value of partly finished goods at the end of the year and the value of the finished goods inventory at the beginning and the end of the year. The result is our cost of goods sold.

The complete departmental budget would include a projected income statement based on the value of the finished goods sold or transferred to other business units for sale. It might also include expense items, unless accounting chooses to count all manufacturing costs as costs of goods sold and not expenses. And accounting may make some adjustments if it wants to assign a portion of total corporate overhead to your department.

Of course, exact procedures and methods will vary at different companies. It's always good to check with and learn from your accounting department. But this chapter has given you the basics you need to create a production budget for your business and helped you learn the accounting terms and ideas most useful to you as a manager.

Manager's Checklist for Chapter 4

- ❑ Numbers come from decisions and actions, not from other numbers.
- ❑ Use past figures as a guide to what has happened in the past. Figure out (or decide) what will happen in the future and generate your numbers from your plan.
- ❑ Income is usually harder to estimate than expenses. Your income is based on decisions *your customers* make and is largely outside your control. Your expenses are based on decisions *you* make and are more under your control.
- ❑ Be careful using percentages in your estimation process. Use them only when there is sound thinking behind the percentages. Even in those cases, look for other factors that may change your estimates.
- ❑ Work in the details. Split line items if you need to. Look at each line item from several viewpoints. At a larger level, build the budget in several pieces and then put it together.
- ❑ If you're responsible for inventory, take the time to learn it well. Learn from experts at your company who can tell you how it's done there. Keep in mind the difference between *physical* inventory and *book* inventory.
- ❑ Use the method for building a manufacturing budget any time you're putting together a budget for manufacturing or assembly or trying to calculate cost of goods sold.

5

Planning and Budgeting a Project

Measure twice, cut once.
—folk saying

Anything we do just once is a project. Projects are harder to budget because we can't really use past figures. Even if we did something similar in the past, prices have changed, the way we work has changed, and our goal is different than last time, too. So we need a budget based on what we plan to do this time, not based on what we did before. We create our project plan and budget in three steps:

- We define the project.
- We create the work plan.
- We calculate the cost.

The key issue in project management is this: we want to get something done and we've never done it before. We're creating a new product or service and we want it to be good, to be of high quality. But we want it done soon and we have limited money. Making the right thing, and making it as good as we can

Use Project Planning the First Time You Do Anything

If you're starting a new production effort, use a project plan for the first cycle. It will give you the best possible estimate and budget. After you've done it once, you'll have a budget for comparison next time. After you've done it three or four times, you'll have a production work plan ironed out.

For example, many students in my project management class have been asked to create a quarterly corporate magazine or newsletter. They use project management for the first three issues, until they know how to do the work well and are ready to make a production schedule and budget.

within a limited schedule and budget, is the art of project management.

Define the Project

Writing a project plan is essential. Without a written plan, we can't be sure that everyone has agreed to do the same thing. By filling out the Quick Project Overview template in Tables 5-1 and 5-2, we get everyone on the same page. Table 5-1 gives an overview with field definitions. Table 5-2 (pages 76-77) is a blank table that you can copy.

Project Name: Descriptive name that indicates project purpose to all parties.

Project Requested by: Customer

Project Manager: IT manager of project

Imposed Budget: Dollar amount desired or required by customer

Underline One:

required limit	desired limit	not yet set

Imposed Delivery Date: Delivery date desired or required by customer

Underline One:

required	desired	not yet set

Table 5-1. Quick project overview with field definitions (continued on next page)

Estimated Cost: Cost estimate from project team

Estimated Delivery Date: Delivery date estimate from project team

Purpose (Justification): The reason the company, or a part of the company, should do the project. The value added to the company by the project. The business justification. The return on investment.

Initial Situation: The starting point. Description of the current system and the problem to be solved.

Current Situation: A status description of where the project is today. This is updated regularly during the project. Current situation = Initial Situation plus Completed Steps.

Goal (Detailed Description): The desired final state when the project is complete and the product is in use and supported. A careful, detailed, but non-technical description of what the system will do, who will use it, and how it will be supported.

Work Plan: Consists of the items listed below.

Concept: Define the idea. Decide if it is worth doing.

Approval

List of tasks to get approval for the Concept Phase.

Analysis: Plan the idea in detail. Know exactly what the customer wants. Decide whether to buy or build.

Approval

List of tasks to get approval for the Analysis Phase.

Design: Figure out exactly what we are making. Plan all the steps of the rest of the project. Create the detailed budget and schedule.

Approval

List of tasks to get approval for the Design Phase.

Development: Do the work. Buy what you need. Put it together. Test it and make sure it works.

Approval

List of tasks to get approval for the Development Phase.

Transition to Production: Create all the manuals and peripherals. Deliver everything to the customer. Train the customer to use it and support it, so they can get value from it without calling you for help.

Approval

Table 5-1. Quick project overview with field definitions (continued)

List of tasks to get approval for the Transition to Production Phase.

Production: The time when the result of your project, the product or service, is in use. Write down what customer service and technical support will do to maintain the product or service in working order.

Decommissioning: Description of events or dates that would cause this product or service to be in need of review for major upgrade or replacement.

Table 5-1. Quick project overview with field definitions (concluded)

We begin by talking to our customers and filling out the top half of the form: purpose, initial situation, and goal. It's important that we get the customer's answers to these questions, and not just our own.

When you take on a project, you're a project manager, even if that's not your job title. A small project may take only a few days and maybe you'll do all the work yourself. That's a good place to start. Over time, you can learn to handle longer projects with more people on them.

Customer Anyone who will use or work with the product or service we create.

Purpose The reason for creating the product or service, its benefit to the organization. How will it help the bottom line? Can we sell it? Will it reduce cost? Will it help us make a better product, serve our customers better, or get things to them sooner? Will it improve safety or reduce risk?

Initial situation The problem to be solved or the opportunity we want to take advantage of. What customers are doing now, what they are using, and why it isn't working. The environment, that is, all of the things with which the new product or service will interact.

Goal What are we making? Picture the end result, the product or service in use by customers. Who are they? What will they be doing? What will they be using?

Imposed Requested or required by the customer. "Imposed" is the opposite of "estimated." "Imposed" is what the customer wants; "estimated" is what we think it will take to do the job.

Project Name:

Project Requested by:

Project Manager:

Imposed Budget: $

Underline One:

required limit	desired limit	not yet set

Imposed Delivery Date:

Underline One:

required	desired	not yet set

Estimated Cost: $

Estimated Delivery Date:

Purpose (Justification):

Initial Situation:

Current Situation:

Goal (Detailed Description):

Work Plan:

-

Table 5-2. Quick project overview, blank for copying (continued on next page)

Concept:
Approval
Analysis:
Approval
Design:
Approval
Development:
Approval
Transition to Production:
Approval
Production:
Decommissioning:

Table 5-2. Quick project overview, blank for copying (continued)

We use the Project Overview to accomplish the first two steps. As we do, we may be told, "This project has to be done by June 1" or "We can only spend $500 on decorations and catering for the big gallery opening." We need to listen to and respect the customers' wishes. We call these the "imposed schedule" and "budget." We aren't saying that we can do what they've asked; but we know they want it. If their request, the imposed date or budget, doesn't match our estimate of what the job will take, we'll work it out with them.

Here are the steps for defining the project and finishing the top half of the Quick Project Overview.

1. Write down what you know. Put question marks next to what you don't know.
2. Talk to people. Find out what they want and get their ideas. Use the overview as a questionnaire; don't leave the meeting without asking at least one question that will help fill in each spot on the top half of the form. If they don't

> **The Six Keys to Project Success**
>
> If a project manager does these six things well, the project is sure to succeed!
>
> 1. Communicate. Listen to everyone involved. Learn what each person wants and what matters to him or her. Talk to everyone. Keep everyone informed and focused on the goal.
> 2. Organize, coordinate, and plan everything. Create a written project overview and work plan.
> 3. Create a detailed work plan. Our schedule and budget come from this.
> 4. Use written change control. If anything changes, write it down and make sure everyone knows. Otherwise, you may end up creating a product with the head of a horse and the tail of a donkey. (And guess what you'll look like in the end!)
> 5. Ensure high quality. Make sure everyone does good work and delivers on time.
> 6. Follow through with quality. Deliver to the customers and make sure that everything works and that they're smiling.

know the answer, ask them who does or if they can find out.

3. Write up what you have and show it to everyone in draft form. Make sure they understand that you want more suggestions and any corrections.
4. Write up their replies. Create a final project overview. Resolve any disagreements.
5. Get approval.

If you do this, your Quick Project Overview (QPO) will look something like the top half of Table 5-3 (pages 79-84) which is a QPO for a quarterly newsletter for a small business.

We complete the QPO by creating the work plan and then estimating our budget.

Create the Work Plan

In a project, the budget and schedule are created from the work plan. Until we know what we're doing, we can't know how much it will cost or how long it will take. A good work plan is the basis

Project Name: Customer Delights! Newsletter

Project Requested by: Owner

Project Manager: Customer Service Manager

Imposed Budget: $500
Underline One: desired limit

Imposed Delivery Date: 10/1/2003
Underline one required

Estimated Cost: $ not yet set

Estimated Delivery Date: 9/25/2003

Purpose (Justification):
We can increase sales by letting our customers know what we are doing and by telling them about our new decorator items and services. Employees coming into the company don't understand our customers and need to learn to focus on the customer. Having them read (and contribute to) Customer Delights! will help.

Initial Situation:
We are growing quickly as a company. The owner used to know every customer personally and call each one two or three times a year. Now, we are too big for that. We need a way to remind our customers of the beauty we bring to their lives so they will come back again. Also, some employees are still learning to keep a focus on delighting our customer. We want them to see success stories and get ideas in how to serve our customers better.

Current Situation:
August 11, 2003: We've decided to create the newsletter. The customer service manager has talked to everyone, gotten in touch with our advertising designer, and found a printer. This plan has been prepared.

Goal (Detailed Description):
On October 1, our customers will find our beautiful four-color, 16-page, 5"x8" Customer Delights! magazine in their mailbox or pick one up when they come by any of our three stores. They will see photos of other customers' homes (or maybe their own home) made beautiful by our decorators. They will have a 10% discount coupon for anything they buy before December 15 and a preview of our holiday gift items. Every employee will receive a copy with a note hand-signed by

Table 5-3. Sample quick project overview for Customer Delights! first issue (continued on pages 80 to 84)

the owner asking them to read the newsletter and think of new ways of delighting our customers. A new edition will come out the first of February, May, August, and October every year.

Work Plan

Concept:

Interview owner, get core idea
Talk to all managers, add new ideas
Talk to favorite customers (friends of the store) and get their reaction
Draft top half of QPO
Run it by managers for suggestions
Revise QPO
- Approval
  - Present QPO to owners
  - Answer any questions
  - Make revisions
  - Owner approves plan

Analysis

Look at our other advertising for ideas
Look at competitors' mailings, newsletters, and catalogs
Meet with advertising consultant, build a mock-up
- Create feature article title and outline
- Create two short article titles and ideas
- Find possible writers
- Select sample images (just to get general idea—may change later)
- Make a list of departments (1-2 paragraphs)
- Convince managers to write department articles

Show mock-up and QPO to managers
Revise
Show mock-up to friends of the store
Revise
Prepare distribution plan
- Discuss printing and delivery schedule with printer
- Arrange for bulk mail
- Write distribution plan

Meet with business manager to go over QPO, distribution plan, and mock-up in detail
Proofread and revise all items
- Approval
- Present entire package to owner

Revise if necessary
Get approval from owner

Design

- Make an exact list of articles and departments
  - Include these items on the list:
  - Title and outline or description
    - Length (in words)
    - Author
    - Alternate author, unless first is committed
- Compose a writing tip sheet
- Plan artwork
  - Go through mock-up, define size and topic of each image
  - Decide color schemes for each 2-page spread
  - Create list of requirements for images
  - Review with advertising consultant, revise with him
  - Proofread and finish artwork plan
- Plan schedule
  - Complete Work Plan (using WBS method later in this chapter)
  - Estimate time for each task
  - Check with graphic artist, advertiser, and printer; confirm they can meet schedule
- Estimate cost
  - Work out prices with
    - Graphic artist
    - Advertiser
    - Printer
      - For materials
      - For printing
      - For bulk mail
      - For delivery
- Prepare budget (Follow *Budgeting for Managers* steps)
- Approval
  - Bring entire package and plan to owner
  - Get suggestions for improvement
  - Revise
  - Get approval from owner

Development

- Inform all vendors and authors we are going ahead
  - Call them (increases enthusiasm)

- Follow up by e-mail or inter-office mail, delivering detailed instructions from work plan
- For each article:
  - Assign to author, sending article description and writing tip sheet
  - Author drafts
  - Review draft
  - Revise (or have author revise)
  - Get author's approval
  - For feature and two major articles
    - Check with owner
    - Revise if necessary
- For images (split the work with advertising consultant and check each other's work)
  - Select a range of images from our photo collection
  - Create 2-page layouts with montages
  - Coordinate colors
  - Check image with text, if text is ready
  - Mark for cropping
- Graphics art preparation
  - Crop images
  - Adjust shading and tone
- Newsletter layout (graphic artist)
  - Enter all articles in word processor
  - Deliver all articles to graphic artist in electronic form
  - Lay out text and graphics
  - Prepare camera-ready copy
- Print galley from camera-ready copy
- Check galleys
  - Proofread text
  - Advertising consultant check images and overall look and feel
  - Review with some managers, whoever is available
  - Make final changes
  - Prepare final mock-up
- Have accounting cut down payment check for printer
  - Approval
    - Show final mock-up at managers' meeting
    - Get revisions (if any) from owner and managers
    - Make changes (if any)
    - Get owner's final approval

Transition to Production

Send to printer
- Camera-ready layout
- Schedule
- Down payment
- Approval

Prepare mailing
- Prepare final mailing list (include self to make sure it went out)
- Review and revise
- Send to printer in electronic format, per printer's bulk mail specification
- Send list of store addresses and shipping quantities

Printer prints

Review printed catalog
- Check one thoroughly
- Check several from different parts of run for color consistency, depth of color
- Request reprint or approve shipping
- Take one box back to headquarters

Printer ships

Completion
- Receive newsletter in mail
- Pay
  - graphic artist
  - advertising consultant
  - printer
- Write up suggestions for doing a better job next time
- Prepare brainstorming meeting for new ideas for the newsletter
- Share at managers' meeting
- Call everyone and thank them, asking friends of the company what they think
- Prepare plan for next issue

Production

Keep in stock at stores

Get employee comments

Over time, design methods for evaluating effectiveness, change as needed

Help managers improve writing skills

Follow up on these ideas (suggested, but not included in first issue):

E-mail version
Large print version for visually impaired
Custom versions for different audiences through smart printing

Decommissioning

Each issue is decommissioned in 3 months
Customer Delights! will continue in production as long as it helps sales more than it costs to produce.

of an accurate budget and a schedule we'll be able to keep. If we want to deliver good results on time and within budget, a written project plan is essential!

A work plan, technically called a Work Breakdown Structure (WBS), is just a very good to-do list for everyone on the project. Some people find it easy to make a good to-do list; others can't even write a shopping list. It doesn't matter. We will show you seven steps to creating a great to-do list, steps that work for anyone. (I've used this system for over four years and I've tested it on my wife, who is a wonderful person in many ways, but couldn't keep a shopping list or make a list of what she needed to do before leaving for vacation. Now, she's a college professor, she's planning courses for her students, and she doesn't even mind planning for our vacation while I write this book!)

TRICKS OF THE TRADE

It's Easier to Revise Than to Write

Many people have a hard time writing a good plan or making a good to-do list. Quit trying!

Instead, make a bad plan: write it quickly and just get it done. Then, revise it. Line by line, paragraph by paragraph, read each item and think about it. Is it clear? Is it correct? Could it be better? Can you think of anything else to add? Is there something you don't know that you can find out and put?

Then have someone read it and make suggestions. When others see you're making your best effort, they'll be happy to help.

Next time you look at a well-written plan, or even an article in a magazine or a book in a bookstore, think: the author didn't write well—she or he just revised a lot!

You can do that yourself.

Seven Steps to Creating a Work Plan

1. Make an incomplete list of tasks. Just write down whatever you think of.
2. Complete the list through visualization, plus asking the right questions and using experts. (Don't worry; we'll show you how.)
3. Group the tasks. Each group of tasks delivers one finished result.
4. Put the groups in order. If the output of Step A is used for Step B, put Step A before Step B.
5. Organize the list into a WBS. Add enough detail.
6. Check the list: key questions.
7. Proofread and format the completed list. Add numbers if you want them.

Some of these steps need a bit more explanation. Let's take a look at them. As you read this section, take a look back at Table 5-3. Look at the bottom half, the work plan, and see how it came from this process.

Make an Incomplete List of Tasks

There are two helpful hints here. The first is that a task is a single piece of work done by one person that leads to a deliverable. A deliverable is something that I can give to you. When you get it, you can use it for the next task without calling me or asking me any questions. If we create a good deliverable at the end of each step, then we build a product from solid components. When the customer gets the finished product, it will work without any problems or questions.

How do we plan clear tasks? Each task is work with a result, so write it as a verb followed by a noun. If you want an example, look at the headings of this chapter: Define the Project, Create the Work Plan, Calculate the Cost. Your work plan should be that crisp and clear.

The second hint is that any project has phases—a number or series of ordered jobs that lead to success. The phase names, with brief definitions, are listed in Table 5-1. You can start by writing down some of the steps needed for each phase.

Task A single piece of work done by one person or a small group of people resulting in a *deliverable*. Also called an action or a step.

Deliverable A work result that can be used as input for a later task. It is independent of the person who created it during the first task. For example, if we have milk delivered, we don't have to call the cow before we drink it.

Phase A collection of related tasks that, together, achieve a *milestone*.

Milestone A large set of related, complete deliverables that demonstrate our progress on a project. Every phase ends with a milestone that is approved before the next phase. Large phases may have internal milestones as well.

Complete the List

The best way to do this is to work with someone else. The person who's doing the work will picture what he or she is doing, thinking it through in detail. The other person prompts him or her with questions and writes down the results, so that the worker's concentration isn't interrupted as he or she builds the plan.

When the worker is picturing the work to be done, ask these two questions and write down the answers.

1. Could you do that step right now? If you get anything other than a firm "Yes!" ask, "What would you have to do first?" Write down those steps above the step she or he started with.
2. If the worker says she or he could do a step right now, ask, "What would you do?" Make an indent and write down those detailed steps underneath the main step.

Now, repeat the whole process. Have the person picture every step listed and for each step repeat the two questions.

You might want to ask a more experienced person for help checking or completing the list. This is usually easy. When you present a written plan, you show that you're trying to do a good job. Most experienced people will be happy to help you do better. Experts avoid giving help to people sometimes, but usually because people are basically saying, "Plan my work for me." To

> **Visualization: The Oldest Trick in the Book**
>
> TRICKS OF THE TRADE
>
> Many people think that visualization is some New Age fad. The opposite is true: it's a foundational tool of American business, first used over a hundred years ago by Andrew Carnegie, a great industrialist and one of the richest men of his day. He passed his methods on to Napoleon Hill, whose book, *Think and Grow Rich*, helped millions of people in the 1920s begin to use visualization. The business bestseller of the 1990s still recommends it: Stephen Covey, author of *The Seven Habits of Highly Effective People*, teaches, "Everything is created twice, first in the mind."
>
> Picture it. Plan it. Do it!

respect an expert, use his or her time well. Just ask for a quick check of your own plan and you may get more help than you expected!

Grouping the Tasks and Putting the Groups in Order

By adding detailed steps, you've already started to create groups of steps. By asking, "What do you have to do first?" you've begun to put the list in a good order. Now, define the result of each group of steps: is it clear what you will deliver? Ask if you have everything you need to start each step. If not, add or move other steps above that one so that you'll have everything you need at the start of each step.

Add Enough Detail

For larger projects, we want to make sure that the smallest tasks (the ones that are furthest indented on our list) are small enough to do in a day or two or maybe a week. We might have a list with three or five indented levels; we want just enough detail so that we can keep track of things.

Check the List: Key Questions

We want to check our list to make sure we aren't missing anything. We begin by looking at each step. Is it clear? Is it a verb followed by a noun? Do we know exactly what we're doing and what we'll deliver?

Next, we walk through each group of steps. If we do each step, in order, will we reach the desired result? Is anything missing? Last, we repeat that with larger groups of steps, walking through every milestone to see that we get the job done with nothing missing. We can think of milestones as steppingstones we use to cross a river: Are all the stones there? Are they firm (clearly defined and not wobbly)? If so, we can cross to our goal on the other side.

Proofreading, Formatting, and Numbering

When our work plan is all done, we'll want to check for spelling errors and clarity. We might also want to add numbers to each step. The numbering system matches the levels of the outline. The big items on the margin are numbered 1, 2, 3 .... Under each item, we have secondary numbers. For example, the items indented under item 2 are numbered 2.1, 2.2, 2.3 .... If we have a third level under some items, we start a third numbering series beginning, for example, with 2.3.1. Renumbering can be a pain, even when using an automated outline numbering system, so it's best to add the numbers when the list is done and is unlikely to change.

This chapter is almost finished and we haven't talked about our project budget yet. This actually makes sense. Project budgets come from project work. Most project budget errors are really the result of incomplete work plans. If the plan is correct and complete, then the budget is easy to make, as we'll see in the next section.

Calculate the Cost

The estimated cost of a project is the cost of the work to be done plus the cost of whatever we need to buy to do it.

Our first step is to estimate the time it takes to do each task. We ask the worker how long it will take to do each task. It's good to ask for a minimum and maximum and then pick something a little above the middle. If the worker has never done the task before, add some extra time. Once we know how long each task will take, we can add up the times and get the total project work hours for each person. If we get the hourly rate from Human Resources, we'll know the cost of labor. Often, we don't count the cost of labor for small projects inside one department.

This also begins to build our project schedule or project calendar, which is a timeline saying who will do each job and when he or she will do it. There's a lot more involved in creating a project schedule than we can fit into this book. If you want to learn more, look for a project management book or class, such as my Project Success™ series, available at www.qualitytechnology.com. Table 5-4, the Project Budget Summary, breaks that down a little further.

How do we use Table 5-4 (page 90) to create a purchasing plan and budget? For each of the four rows, we ask what we'll need for each task listed on the WBS.

Table 5-5 (page 91) shows the project budget for the first issue of Customer Delights! For this project, internal staff time was not considered a project expense.

Normally, we would not include the last column, "Type of Item." We added it here to show you how we thought through the project plan. As an exercise, compare this budget with the work plan in Table 5-3. If I missed anything, send me an e-mail!

Tracking a Project

In this chapter, we've done a lot more than just help you make a budget. We've helped you plan a whole project. You can track project work done, time, and costs with the tools you see here. For a simple project where you aren't counting work time, you can simply write "done" and a date next to each item when you finish it. If you have a project team, you should run a weekly status meeting and update the list at the meeting. You can follow up on consulting expenses by sending quick e-mails asking if everything is on budget. And you can track purchases through purchase orders. We'll discuss tracking more in Chapter 9.

Work Time	Notes	Method	See Chaps
In-house staff	Often not counted in project costs at departmental level	WBS, estimate time per task, total the results, multiply by rate	3, 10
Consultants and Contractors	Negotiate contracts if possible Use WBS to define job, deliverables, and production schedule	Tasks defined in WBS, get the right people for the job Get bid or estimate from vendor	3
Purchasing			
Direct Materials	For example: photos from advertising consultant; paper, cover stock, and staples included in printer's price quote	Each item from WBS: What do I need to include in the product?	3
Indirect Materials	Includes tools, equipment, and anything used up and disposed of For example: might need to buy a computer program to manage mailing lists	Estimate cost, get bids for large items	3

Table 5-4. The Project Budget Summary

Manager's Checklist for Chapter 5

- ❑ Always create a project plan first, then build the estimate and budget from the plan.
- ❑ Projects without written plans fail: people aren't on the same page. Know your purpose, set your goal, and know where you're starting and what problem you're trying to solve.
- ❑ Remember the six keys to project success. If you do lots of projects, make a copy and put it on your desk.
- ❑ Teach everyone on your team how to plan their work with visualization plus questions.
- ❑ A project budget has four elements: cost of internal labor,

Phase Item	Quantity	Unit Cost	Cost	Type of Item
Concept				
Coffee hour for friends of the store			$75	Indirect materials
Analysis				
Meeting with ad consultant (per hour)	3	$150	$450	Consulting labor
	2	$150	$300	Consulting labor
Design				
Ad consultant reviews artwork plan	1	$150	$150	Consulting labor
Development				
Image development	8	$150	$1,200	Consulting labor
Newsletter layout	16	$75	$1,200	Consulting labor
Check galleys	1	$150	$150	Consulting labor
Transition to Production				
Software to prepare bulk mailing	1	$129	$129	Indirect materials
Printing (per copy)	2,000	$1.50	$3,000	Direct materials and service
Bulk mailing (per customer)	1,500	$0.50	$750	Services
Shipping			$50	Services
Total			**$7,454**	

Table 5-5. A Sample Project Budget: Customer Delights!

cost of consulting and similar services, cost of direct materials, and cost of indirect materials and tools.

❑ An accurate budget comes from a detailed work plan.

6

Checking It Twice

He's making a list, he's checking it twice.
—J. Fred Coots and Haven Gillespie

Mistakes are easy to make and hard to find. They last a long time if we don't catch them. (In fact, in researching the line from "Santa Claus Is Coming to Town" above, we found that it's attributed not only to Haven but also to Henry. That is a mistake that has been passed around to dozens of places.) We should do our best to eliminate mistakes, big and small, from our budget. If we understand where errors come from, we can establish methods that prevent errors or catch them before it's too late.

Using a Partner for Proofreading

No matter how good a job we think we can do, we all make mistakes. Even computer programmers, who work to be as precise as they can, create one new error for every five they fix. Worse, when we read what we wrote, we tend to see what we think we wrote, and not what's actually there. We need to have others check what we do. See the sidebars for two approaches (and a caution).

Errors Created by Spreadsheet Programs

Some people might think, "I can skip this chapter: I use a spreadsheet program and it doesn't make mistakes." Unfortunately, that's simply not true.

When we change tools, we change the types of errors we make, but we don't get rid of errors. With word processors and spell-checkers, we make fewer spelling errors than we did with typewriters and dictionaries. But we make more errors of using the wrong word, because the spell-checker can't catch those.

> **Mistake Proofing**
>
> ### Reading Aloud Catches Errors
>
> When you have complex tables, you can have someone read your work aloud to you while you check it against another copy. The other reader will read what he or she sees and you'll hear errors that you couldn't see. If you say "OK" every time a number is right and the other person says, "Next line" every time he or she goes to a new line, you can create a rhythm and go very quickly.

It's the same with spreadsheet programs. There are fewer addition errors, but there are more errors of other types: errors in formulas, inserted columns that throw off our totals, and other such things.

Spreadsheets can even make addition errors. Take a look at columns A1 and B1 in Table 6-1, which was copied directly from an Excel spreadsheet. Then, check the addition yourself. Which column is right?

> **Smart Managing**
>
> ### The "Everything Gets Checked" Office Policy
>
> Some people think that if we want to check their work, we think they aren't doing a good job. To depersonalize this issue and show people that we get better results by accepting help and working together, try this. Make a rule that two people see everything before it leaves the department. Start by having people read what you write and correct it for you. When your team sees that you want help (and they find a few dumb mistakes you've made), they'll be willing to receive help as well. Of course, you should make a policy appropriate to your department's workload. Perhaps you don't check every e-mail, but you check letters, tax forms, purchase orders, and legal documents.

For Example

An Error Etched in Stone

Even after being a writer and editor for over 20 years, I still make proofreading mistakes. One time, I needed to verify the etching for a tombstone. I checked it five times and had my wife check it as well. Everything looked fine and we approved it. Well, the name was spelled right. But, unfortunately, the word "niece" was misspelled. I'd written it wrong in the original, but I assumed that the stone carvers checked the ordinary words, so I'd checked only the names.

Make sure your errors are fixed before they are etched in stone—or in the annual budget.

	A1	B1	A2	B2
	Estimated	Estimated with Rounding	Estimated	Estimated with Rounding
Expenses				
Equipment leases	$200.00	$200.00	$200.0000	$200.0000
Toner	90.00	90.00	90.0000	90.0000
Plain paper	30.00	30.00	30.0000	30.0000
Special papers	6.00	6.00	6.0000	6.0000
Equipment purchase	79.17	79.17	79.1667	79.1700
Service contracts	133.33	133.33	133.3333	133.3300
Equipment repair	29.17	29.17	29.1667	29.1700
Miscellaneous	15.00	15.00	15.0000	15.0000
Sales tax	19.95	19.95	19.9467	19.9500
Total Expenses	**$602.61**	**$602.62**	**$602.61**	**$602.62**

Table 6-1. Computer spreadsheet with rounding error

If you check the total, you will find it should be $602.62, not $602.61. Yet the formula in the "Total expenses" cell of column A1 is the sum of the correct line items. What went wrong? It is called a *rounding error*. The numbers in the spreadsheet are not exact figures; each line item is rounded to the nearest cent for display. But, inside the computer file, $79.17 is actually a third of a cent lower, $79.16666. Several of the cells have this error. When they are added, the fractions of a cent add up and the total ends up one cent off. We often get these kinds of errors in estimates, because we create the numbers by dividing other numbers. In this case, the monthly figures were calculated by dividing the annual figures by 12. When the display was adjusted to show cents, the rounding error was hidden.

We can solve this problem with the ROUND() command, which was used in columns B1 and B2. When we use the ROUND() command, the spreadsheet program automatically rounds the figure to the correct decimal place. For instance, 950/12 = 79.16666. But ROUND((950/12),2) = 79.17, an amount in exact cents. We illustrate this by showing columns A2 and B2 with four decimal places.

This may be a small error, but the simple fact that it is wrong can create a lot of embarrassment. In this case, Eric, who has a degree in accounting and an MBA, created the spreadsheet. Then I checked it (and missed the error). Our proofreader, a college student, caught it for us. Being smart doesn't keep us from making mistakes or making bad assumptions. Remember: spreadsheet errors are hard to find. We don't see the formulas, so we can't see if they're wrong.

Spreadsheets can also have very large errors that are hard to find. Here is a common way to create a faulty spreadsheet: If

But They Were Never Right in the First Place

For Example

A number of years ago, a large corporation decided to shift entirely away from the Lotus 1-2-3 spreadsheet program to Microsoft Excel. One department resisted for over three years. That department had built huge estimation tables in Lotus 1-2-3 and said that it would be too difficult to redo all of the spreadsheets in Excel and that errors were sure to creep in. Finally, the corporate executives hired a team of analysts to convert the spreadsheets. They discovered that there were so many errors in the Lotus 1-2-3 spreadsheets that they were really useless. Over the years, people had added rows and columns without carefully checking to see if the formulas were right or wrong. The department had been defending a set of spreadsheets that really didn't work at all. The analysts corrected the errors as they built the new spreadsheets in Excel.

Let's not defend our spreadsheets; let's check them and make sure they're right!

we are making a budget, we may add new line items to the bottom of the list, just above the total. If we aren't careful, we may forget to adjust the total range, so that the new items aren't included. The automatic cross-checking tools in the next section will help you catch these errors.

Automatic Cross-Checking in Spreadsheets

The most common error in a budget spreadsheet is a column or row total that is not adding up all the figures it should be adding up. There are two common causes of this problem.

The first is an inserted row that is not counted in the column totals. This can happen if a row is inserted at the bottom of a column of figures. The total below that list of figures may not include the final row.

The second common cause of budget spreadsheet errors is copying formulas without checking them to make sure that the formulas are now adding the correct cells. We may find that the total at the bottom of one column is actually adding up a different column. For example, we may have the total at the bottom of the February column adding up the figures for January.

There is a simple, automatic way to catch these errors, as illustrated in Tables 6-2 and 6-3.

In Table 6-2, columns B, C, and D are each totaled on row 6 and rows 2 through 5 are totaled in column E. Cell E6 at the bottom of the total column should come out the same, whether

A	B	C	D	E	F
1	January	February	March	Total	
2 Salary	$5,000.00	$5,200.00	$4,400.00	$14,600.00	
3 Utilities	$500.00	$200.00	$450.00	$1,150.00	
4 Insurance	$250.00	$250.00	$250.00	$750.00	
5 Printing	$300.00	$100.00	$450.00	$850.00	
6 Total	$6,050.00	$5,750.00	$5,550.00	$17,350.00	$17,350.00
7					$—

Table 6-2. Spreadsheet error checking, example

it is the total of the columns or the total of the rows. But, if there's an error in the spreadsheet formulas, there would be a difference. We can make use of this by totaling both the columns and the rows and seeing if the two grand totals match.

> Key Term
>
> **Checksum** A method of finding errors by comparing two different totals of the same figures.
>
> **Checksum column** A column in a spreadsheet that contains only checksum formulas.

Table 6-3 shows the formulas that set up automatic checking. Cell E6 contains the sum of the three columns. Cell F6 contains the sum of the four rows. Below that, cell F7 contains the difference between the two totals. If that difference is zero, then the two totals are the same and we can be reasonably sure that each row and column total is correct and contains the correct formula. If the value in F7 is not zero, then we need to check each formula to find the error(s). When we correct the error(s), F7 will recalculate to zero.

> Tricks of the Trade
>
> **Don't Print Your Checksum Column**
>
> We've designed the spreadsheet so that Column F contains only formulas for checking the spreadsheet. The results of those formulas don't need to be seen in printed copies of your budget. There are two easy ways to hide your checksum column. First, when you create print ranges, don't include the checksum column. Second, if people are going to view your spreadsheet in electronic format, you can use the Column Hide function to hide the checksum column or columns.

Table 6-4 shows us what an error will look like in our error checking formula. Cell F7 shows us that the two totals are different, by $200. As an exercise, make this spreadsheet yourself and see if you can recreate the error and then correct it.

Document Version Control

If you use checksums in your spreadsheets and have someone check your work closely, there's a pretty good chance that each

A	B	C	D	E	F
1	January	February	March	Total	
2 Salary	$5,000.00	$5,200.00	$4,400.00	SUM(B2:D2)	
3 Utilities	$500.00	$200.00	$450.00	SUM(B3:D3)	
4 Insurance	$250.00	$250.00	$250.00	SUM(B4:D4)	
5 Printing	$300.00	$100.00	$450.00	SUM(B5:D5)	
6 Total	SUM(B2:B5)	SUM(C2:C5)	SUM(D2:D5)	SUM(B6:D6)	SUM(E2:E5)
7					E6–F6

Table 6-3. Spreadsheet error checking, formulas

A	B	C	D	E	F
1	January	February	March	Total	
2 Salary	$5,000.00	$5,200.00	$4,400.00	$14,600.00	
3 Utilities	$500.00	$200.00	$450.00	$1,150.00	
4 Insurance	$250.00	$250.00	$250.00	$750.00	
5 Printing	$300.00	$100.00	$450.00	$850.00	
6 Total	$6,050.00	$5,750.00	$5,750.00	$17,550.00	$17,350.00
7					$200.00

Table 6-4. Spreadsheet error checking, example of an error

spreadsheet you create will be error-free. But a budget is more than just one spreadsheet.

There are three more very common mistakes you need to prevent. The first mistake is completing a budget, but then sending an earlier version instead of the final, correct version. The second mistake is having several spreadsheets and budget documents and not checking to make sure that they match. You may make sure they match, but then change one and forget to change the other. The third mistake is allowing two people to make changes to the same document at the same time. If you do this, you end up with two different documents, and it's a real pain to combine the two to include changes from both editors.

You prevent these problems with good *version control*,

Version control A system for making sure that you have the recent version of any item, with everyone's changes and corrections.

Document control Version control for documents such as budgets and budgetary assumptions.

Document control system A computer document management system that ensures that only one person can change a document at a time and that the latest version of the document is delivered. It can also include ways of marking who made each change to a document.

which, when applied to documents, is called *document control.* One simple approach is to include the filename of each document in the document and to include the date of the last change in the filename. You can also use automated tools, such as the Track Changes function in Microsoft Word. And perhaps your company has a document control system installed.

It's essential to be aware of the issues and to create a simple and effective solution. Here are some ideas:

Make sure everyone on your team has read this chapter and is aware of the problems. When a mistake occurs, use it—with no blame—to show how these things happen to everyone and how you can prevent them through good procedures.

Make a simple spreadsheet page that lists every document in your budget by filename and title. Then, in the columns to the right, put in a series of steps, such as "draft," "review," "revise," "proofread," and "print." Whenever one of these steps is done, the person who does it can put his or her initials and the date into the box next to the document.

On each file, put a date in the filename in the format YYYYMMDD. For example, October 3, 2002 is 20021003. Then the files will sort in date order, with the newest file last.

When you have multiple spreadsheets, you can put them all in one file, using multiple worksheets in a single file. You can also create links across spreadsheet pages by using formulas that copy cells from one worksheet to another. If you do this, you need to be very careful. It's easy to set up these spreadsheets, but it's very hard to make sure you've copied the right cell. Formulas that copy information from one worksheet to another need to be checked several times, both on the screen and also in print.

Verifying Budgetary Assumptions

Once all of your spreadsheets are checked and correct, you need to verify that the budgetary assumptions are accurate and appropriate.

Here are some things you should do to check your budgetary assumptions:

- Have someone read the budgetary assumptions for clarity and ask you to revise anything he or she doesn't understand.
- Have someone proofread the budgetary assumptions, paying close attention to the names and locations of documents and sources.
- Use a buddy-check to make sure that each assumption is

MISTAKE PROOFING

The Later, the Better

When creating links between spreadsheets or copying figures from one spreadsheet to another, it's best to finish each spreadsheet and check it thoroughly before you create formulas that link worksheets or copy the data from one worksheet to another. That way, there will be fewer changes to spreadsheets and less chance that errors will creep in.

TRICKS OF THE TRADE

Less Is More

Most new managers want to explain their thinking for every line of the budget. As a general rule, however, the financial department wants very few comments. Professional accountants document only those items that are unusual, don't follow standard accounting procedures, or have to account for missing information.

If you want to check your own work carefully, you can write out a list of your own methods and steps. You might make notes about which items were estimated from past figures, which were estimated from work plans, and who you talked to. But, when it comes to presenting budgetary assumptions, you might present only two or three of the dozen or more notes that you made.

correctly linked to the right line of a spreadsheet and that any figures in the budgetary assumptions match the figures in the spreadsheet.

The Final Proofreading Steps

When you think everything is ready, you need to do three last checks:

- Before you print, check for correct page numbers, headers, footers, title pages, and notes or appendices.
- After you print, do a buddy-check to compare the starting numbers for this year or period and the closing numbers from last year or the last period.
- After you print, let everything sit overnight and look at it in the morning. With fresh eyes, you can catch the mistakes that you hadn't noticed—like a misspelling of the company's name on the title page.

If you need to make a presentation of your budget at a meeting, then you may want to add a slide show or charts and diagrams. We'll take a look at that in Chapter 7, Preparing for Presentation.

Manager's Checklist for Chapter 6

- ❑ Everyone makes mistakes—and it's very hard to find your own mistakes.
- ❑ Make a rule that everyone's work (especially your own) is checked by someone else.
- ❑ Use checksums and checksum columns in your spreadsheets.
- ❑ Use a system for document version control. If your company doesn't have one, set up a simple set of checklists and filenames with dates for your department.
- ❑ Link spreadsheets after each spreadsheet is complete and correct. This prevents errors from creeping in.

- ❏ Cross-check all spreadsheets against each other with buddy-checking.
- ❏ Double-check budgetary assumptions and your entire document before you deliver.
- ❏ Make sure you print and deliver the final version of your budget, not an earlier version.

7

Preparing for Presentation

It ain't over till the fat lady sings.

—Anonymous

Creating a budget involves a lot of detailed work. While we're making the budget, most of our attention is on thinking carefully, calculating correctly, and getting the figures right. And that's exactly what we should be doing. However, when we've finished getting all the parts right and all the details correct, we need to change our focus. We need to take a look at the whole package, think about our audience, and decide how to present the budget.

Here are the skills you will learn in this chapter:

- Combining parts of your budget
- Revising budgetary assumptions
- Creating templates and formatting a budget
- Adding account codes
- Preparing a budget presentation

Combining Parts of Your Budget

In a busy department, your team is likely to be doing many things at once. It's quite possible that the best way to build a budget is to estimate each activity separately, using the best estimation method for each activity, and then create a budget for each of them. To put together the departmental budget, we then combine all the activity budgets into one. This approach is especially useful if some of the department's activities operate on a production basis, using the estimation methods illustrated in Chapters 1, 3, and 4, and other activities are managed as projects, using the estimation methods from Chapter 5.

To illustrate this, let's look at more details of Robert's information technology department budget, an example we introduced in Chapter 1. Robert needs to plan the budget for the coming year for computer support, new computers for staff, and installing the new warehouse inventory system. The budgets for these three activities are in Tables 7-1, 7-2, and 7-3. Robert is not responsible for salaries, so we'll see an expense budget without salaries.

Table 7-1 is Robert's budget for the routine annual work of the department. He prepared the estimate by looking at the work plans and budgets of the last two years and making a work plan and budget for this year.

Table 7-2 is a project budget for buying and installing new computers for new staff members. He consulted his customer, the Human Resources Department, and learned that the company planned to bring in 10 new people for jobs that would need computers. He then wrote a project plan and created the budget that you see in Table 7-2.

Table 7-3 shows the project budget that Robert developed with the help of the subcontractor who will design and install the new inventory computer system.

Now, let's combine all three of these tables into one departmental budget, shown in Table 7-4. The key to doing this well is the account codes. We organize the rows by account code and

Expenses	Account Codes	Year 2003
Replacement Computers	*101*	*$30,000*
Parts		
Monitors	201	$3,000
Hard drives	202	$1,800
Other	210	$1,200
Total Parts	*200*	*$6,000*
Tools	*300*	*$800*
Supplies		
Computer cleaning	401	$1,000
Other	410	$500
Total Supplies	*400*	*$1,500*
Shipping	*800*	*$1,200*
Sales Tax	*900*	*$2,625*
Expense Total		**$42,125**

Table 7-1. Computer support expenses

Expenses	Account Codes	Year 2003
New Computers	*102*	*$15,000*
Parts		
Monitors	201	$900
Hard Drives	202	$1,500
Other	210	$500
Total Parts	*200*	*$2,900*
Shipping	*800*	*$400*
Sales Tax	*900*	*$1,253*
Expense Total		**$19,553**

Table 7-2. New staff computer project budget

the columns by budget. Then we enter and total the numbers, as described in the instructions below.

Table 7-4 illustrates all of the steps for consolidating a budget except #10, putting in cross-check calculations. We leave this as an exercise for you. Pay close attention to the discounts that appear only in the totals column.

Expenses	Account Codes	Year 2003
Warehouse Server	*104*	*$12,000*
Warehouse Computers	*103*	*$7,500*
Parts		
Graphics Monitors	203	$1,000
Total Parts	*200*	*$1,000*
Specialized Software	*501*	*$30,000*
Subcontractor Services		
Analysis and Design	601	$20,000
Development	602	$15,000
Installation	603	$7,000
Total Subcontractor Services	*600*	*$42,000*
Sales Tax	*900*	*$3,535*
Expense Total		**$96,035**

Table 7-3. New inventory computer system project

Where did those discounts come from, by the way? The sidebar, "Saving Money Through Careful Planning," will show you. Table 7-4 is a detailed consolidation budget, showing all of the figures. Later in this chapter, we will show you how to trim it down to size for different presentations.

Consolidating Budgets

Here are the key steps for creating a consolidated budget from several smaller budgets.

1. List all of the account codes in Column B, with a code for the group total beneath each group.
2. List the account groups and line items (sub-accounts) in Column A.
3. Create a column for each budget you are consolidating.
4. To the right of those columns, create a total column.
5. Copy numbers from each sheet to the appropriate column, making sure to match line item numbers.
6. Total each line item across.
7. Total each group down.
8. Put a grand total at the bottom.
9. Put in appropriate cross-check calculations to verify this spreadsheet to its source spreadsheets.

A	B	C	D	E	F
Expenses	**Account Codes**	**Support**	**New Computers**	**Warehouse Project**	**Year 2003**
Computers					
Replacement Computers	101	$30,000			$30,000
New Computers	102		$15,000		$15,000
Warehouse Computers	103			$7,500	$7,500
Warehouse Servers	104			$12,000	$12,000
Computers Subtotal					$64,500
Less bulk purchase discount (4%)	191				-$2,580
Total Computers	**100**				**$61,920**
Parts					
Monitors	201	$3,000	$900		$3,900
Hard Drives	202	$1,800	$1,500		$3,300
Graphics Monitors	203			$1,000	$1,000
Other	210	$1,200	$500		$1,700
Total Parts	***200***				**$9,900**
Tools					
Total Tools	**300**	$800			**$800**
Supplies					
Computer Cleaning	401	$1,000			$1,000
Other	410	$500			$500
Total Supplies	**400**				**$1,500**
Specialized Software					
Inventory Software	501			$30,000	$30,000
Total Specialized Software	**500**				**$30,000**
Subcontractor Services					
Analysis and design	601			$20,000	$20,000
Development	602			$15,000	$15,000
Installation	603			$7,000	$7,000
Total Subcontractor services	**600**				**$42,000**
Shipping					
Total Shipping	**800**	**$1,200**	**$400**		**$1,600**
Sales Tax					
Sales Tax	901	$2,625	$1,253	$3,535	$7,413
Adjustment due to discount	991				-$103
Total Sales Tax	**900**				**$7,310**
Total Computer Department Budget					**$155,030**

Table 7-4. Computer department consolidated budget

Revising Budgetary Assumptions

As you work on the details of your budget, it's good to take notes and keep track of your thinking. Initially, you write notes

Saving Money Through Careful Planning

When Robert was working with the consultant to create the project budget for the inventory system, the consultant mentioned that it was too bad that Robert needed only five computers for the warehouse. If he needed 10 or more, then the vendor could give a discount for bulk purchase. Robert had chosen to buy all the same brand of computers for upgrades, new purchases, and the inventory system, because that reduces maintenance costs. He realized that if he ordered all the computers from the vendor who was supplying the consultant for the inventory project, he could get the discount. And, with the discount, sales tax would also go down.

Robert did more than consolidate his budget on paper. He consolidated the purchase orders, saving his company $2,683.

about your thinking only to yourself. You should review them by asking the question, "Will I understand this note a year from now when I need to make a new budget?" If yes, then the note in the spreadsheet is just fine.

However, when it comes time to finish your budget for presentation, you may want to write it up quite differently. First, you should ask the accounting department for examples of the budgetary assumptions that they like to see. Second, you should ask your boss what he or she wants to see.

It is likely that they will want to see different things. The financial department will want to see relatively few assumptions, as accountants and financial managers use the budgetary assumptions page only to identify things that are out of the ordi-

Use Spreadsheet Comments for Budgetary Assumptions

If you're using Microsoft Excel or a similar spreadsheet program, an excellent way to take notes is to use the cell comment feature. If you choose a cell with the mouse pointer and right-click, you can access a menu that includes the *Insert Comment* command. When you insert a comment, a tiny triangle in the upper right corner of the cell shows the comment and the comment pops up in a small text box to show the note we've written. Once a comment is in place, the right-click menu gives us new options: show, edit, or delete.

nary, such as unusual methods or missing information. Your boss, on the other hand, is likely to want to know where you got your numbers and what you will be using the money for. So, you may want to prepare two different pages of budgetary assumptions for your two audiences.

Here are some other things you should do when you review your notes and put together your page of budgetary assumptions.

Look at each note:

- Is it clear? Could someone other than you understand it?
- Are all references clear? Would someone else know how to find the files or people you're referencing?

Ask if each note will help your audience:

- Will this note help make sense of the budget to others?
- Is this what your audience really wants to know?
- Are you *justifying* what you've done (trying to show you've done a good job) or *explaining* it (telling others what they really need to know)?

Creating Templates and Formatting a Budget

How important is a clear presentation? How important are fonts and underlines? If the figures are right, does appearance really matter?

The answer is that, while getting the numbers right is most important, making the budget look good matters as

Know Your Audience

Smart Managing

I used to think that I had to explain every point of my budget just to show that I was thinking carefully. That wasn't management; that was insecurity. Generally, our bosses will trust us to do good work. The budgetary assumptions we show them should focus on what concerns them: Are we using money well? Are we planning to do all the work we need to get done?

Of course, your boss may want to know the details or there may be an audit of the department. So it makes sense to keep careful notes. Just don't present those notes as budgetary assumptions. Keep them in reserve in case someone asks for them.

Planning the Format of a Budget

There are a number of questions you can ask to decide how you want your budget to look:

- Should totals be directly below the items they total or offset one column to the right?
- Should column headings be bold or italic?
- Should items be bold or italic?
- Should sub-items be bold or italic?
- Should sub-totals be bold, italic, or underlined?
- Should totals be bold, italic, underlined, or double-underlined?
- If you are comparing estimated and actual, do you want estimated in regular font and actual in italic?

well. In a budget, good formatting is not just a matter of making it pretty. A good format is also making it clear. People will understand the budget more easily if the format helps them see the numbers that matter and know what the numbers represent without having to think about the format and layout too much.

What is the best format to use? There's no one right answer. Some companies have predefined spreadsheet formats. If there's a standard at your company, you should follow it. If not, then you can make one yourself. But you might show it to your boss and to accounting. If your boss has been using double underlines for totals for 30 years, then you should do the same, so that she or he can read your budgets easily.

Formats and Templates

Here are some things to do when setting up budget formats and templates:

- Make template files with no numbers in them. Save each template file and copy it to create new budgets.
- Set up spreadsheets with properly formatted columns, totals, formulas, and links that you can use over and over again.
- Use comments to explain complicated formulas.
- If the budget will be photocopied on poor-quality copiers, avoid bold, as it may not be apparent in copies.

Adding Account Codes

When you're presenting the budget to most audiences, you don't need to show account codes. Executives really don't care that the account code for new computer purchases is 102. However, accounting does care. You can put account code numbers in their own rows and columns and hide them before printing except when we give the budget to the accounting department. Then you can reveal the hidden account code columns and rows when you deliver the budget to accounting.

Some Common Errors to Avoid

- Don't adjust formats by typing in spaces. Learn to align cells to the right, left, center, and decimal point. Set items and subitems in separate columns.
- Don't use multiple rows for column headers. Learn to use word wrap when needed.
- Be judicious in your fonts, such as bold, italic, or bold italic. Use them only when emphasis makes the text clearer.

You may also want to show account codes when you're tracking the budget. Invoices and other expense documents will show account codes. If we show account codes while working with them, it's easy to verify that the funds were applied to the correct sub-accounts.

Sometimes, you may need to break out a separate budget presentation for a particular account code. Perhaps a project is running over budget or some funds were misallocated. By creating a separate spreadsheet for the one account code, you can focus on the problem and decide how to resolve it.

There's one other time when account codes are useful. When you're tracking a budget, as described in Chapter 9, you'll want to see the account codes. That way, when you look at an invoice, you can quickly compare the account code with the budget to make sure you're posting the expense to the proper line item.

Preparing a Budget Presentation

When you prepare a budget presentation, you have to change your focus from getting the budget right to making the budget relevant and clear. You need to think about the purpose of the presentation and the interests of your audience. Based on that, you decide what to include, how much to include, how to deal with estimated ranges, and the format for presentation.

A presentation can be as simple as the delivery of a document of two or a few pages. Or it could be best to prepare a slide show using a tool such as Microsoft PowerPoint. In addition to the printed presentation, you should also prepare to give an oral presentation of the budget at a meeting. This helps people understand the work you plan to do and the money you need and gives them a chance to ask questions about anything they do not understand. You may also have to negotiate to get the money you want; we'll discuss that further in Chapter 12.

What to Include for Different Audiences

There are three questions to ask when preparing a budget presentation:

- Who will attend the presentation?
- Why do they want to see the budget? Why do they want to talk to you? What are they concerned about?
- What will the results of the meeting be?

Let's look at each of these in a little more detail.

Who will attend the presentation? Will the audience be composed mostly of executives with a focus on business or of financial and accounting people with a focus on money? If the focus is on business, then the issues will be more about productivity and success. If the focus is on finance, then the issues are more likely to be cost-cutting or financial controls. Financial controls can include such issues as ensuring that the money is spent as planned and that there are few inventory losses or no inappropriate uses of funds.

Why do they want to see the budget? What is the biggest concern? If you're not sure, ask them by phone or email. It is not a problem admitting you don't know; the problem is showing up unprepared. Here are some issues that you can mention when asking the reason for the presentation:

- A routine review to ensure understanding of a budget and work plan that is likely to be approved.
- A close review of a budget and work plan or project plan that is crucial to business success.
- A close review of a budget to see if it can be reduced.
- A competitive review where limited money is distributed to different budgets.

Once you know the purpose of the meeting, you can design a presentation and an agenda to meet the meeting's objectives.

What will the results of the meeting be? Will there simply be a sharing of information and explanations? Or will there be a decision during the meeting or following shortly? Will only the total budgetary amount for the department be decided or will each line item be reviewed? Are a project plan and project goals being reviewed at the same time?

A written agenda makes meetings much easier, espe-

Preparing an Agenda

For every meeting, prepare an agenda and deliver it in advance. An agenda should be one or two pages long. Here is what it should look like:

- At the top, list the date, time, and place of the meeting.
- List everyone who is attending.
- State the purpose and goal of the meeting.
- List all of the activities of the meeting, in this order:
  - –Information items—short things you want to tell everyone that don't require discussion.
  - –Brainstorming items—items for discussion that do not need to be resolved in this meeting (one or two per meeting).
  - –Decision items—topics with clear alternatives to be discussed and a decision to be made (one or two per meeting).
  - –Attach any items (such as your budget) that should be read in advance of the meeting and deliver the agenda at least two days in advance by email or in printed form.

cially when it states a clear goal and asks people to read material in advance. People are more likely to come to the meeting and the meeting is more likely to run on time. You can move through the agenda and finish topics promptly.

How Much to Include

In deciding how much material and detail from your budget to include in a presentation, you should be guided by the purpose of the presentation. There are two main things to consider: scope and level of detail. Scope is the amount of material you cover—an outline of everything to be included in a budget, a department's responsibilities, or a project. Level of detail is the depth of coverage. How much detail is important in a budget presentation? Do you need to show sub-items? Do you need to show small items or do you want to show only items over a certain dollar amount?

In matching the scope of the meeting and the scope of the budget, here are some things to consider:

- If all of the work of your department is being reviewed, then you should include the entire departmental budget.
- If you don't control salary and there are no plans to change staffing levels, then don't include the salary budget.
- If only salary and positions are being reviewed, you don't need to present the expense budget.
- If the meeting is reviewing only a project or only some of your department's work, present a budget only for the work under review at the meeting.

When considering the level of detail of your budget, think both about how much (or how little) information you want to present and about what size dollar figures are really going to matter for the purpose of the meeting. It's best to fit the budget on a single page if you can. One page is much easier to read than pages and pages of detail. Remember that you are familiar with your department and your budget, but that others are read-

> **Using Account Codes to Organize Presentations**
>
> If you know that a particular project or a particular part of your department's work is going to be reviewed or discussed separately, it is a good idea to put all the work of that department under one account code, separate from other activities. That way, it's easy to estimate and track the work separately from the rest of the work of your department.

ing it for the first time. In addition, consider the size of the numbers. For example, if a meeting is looking at whether a project worth tens of thousands of dollars is worth the cost, then details about items worth under a thousand dollars are not going to be very important.

> **Bring Supporting Documents**
>
> If you want to make your presentation short and simple, but you're worried that your figures will be challenged, then here is a good approach: make the presentation short and give just an overview budget in a page or two, but bring two copies of supporting documents—several more pages of detail and explanation. Why bring two copies? So that if people at the meeting want copies, you can have someone run photocopies while you begin to present the details.

What Kinds of Things to Include

The content of your presentation should be what's needed to meet the goal of the meeting. For example, include budgetary assumptions only if this is a financial review, not if this is a review of the business objectives of the work plan. Create a concise, focused presentation of the materials needed to present your case. Include only what is needed—nothing more, nothing less.

When to Offer Ranges vs. Solid Figures

As we discussed in Chapters 1 and 4, a budget is nothing more than a

> **Less Is More**
>
> If your presentation is focused and concise, you're less likely to bore, distract, or encourage members of the audience to go off on tangents.

good guess about the future. As a result, you may want to present a range of estimates, rather than exact figures. Here are some things to consider:

- When there are two ways to present ranges, one is to present a low figure and a high figure; the other is to present a single figure, plus or minus a certain percentage. For example, you can say that an item will range from a low of $9,500 to a high of $10,500 or will be $10,000 plus or minus 5%.
- If figures are the result of doing exactly what you did in the prior year or the result of committed contracts such as leases or purchasing contracts, then exact figures are more suitable than ranges.
- If some figures are exact and some are rough estimates, you can present a budget in two columns, with a minimum estimate in one column and a maximum estimate in another column. If the figure is exact for a given line item, then the same number appears in both columns.
- You can also present a budget in two columns if you have alternate plans. You can present a budget for each plan, so that the people at the meeting can compare the two plans.

As an example of presenting alternate plans, let's take a look at a bidding spreadsheet prepared by Jose, the computer consultant who prepared a bid for the new inventory system and gave it to Robert. You will see the low and high bid proposals in Table 7-5.

Jose accompanied this budget with an explanation of the difference between the two systems. The less expensive system would stand alone and not link into the corporate network. It would work just fine, but only send reports to the main office. It couldn't be updated from the main office. The higher bid is the price for a system that would link into the main office, with an extra software module to make the link and some extra customization that increased design, develop-

Computer Inventory System	Low Bid	High Bid
Server	$12,000	$15,000
Workstations	$7,500	$7,500
Graphics Monitors	$1,000	$2,500
Inventory Software	$30,000	$30,000
Module to link in corporate network	$0	$10,000
Analysis and Design	$20,000	$35,000
Development	$15,000	$25,000
Installation	$7,000	$10,000
Sales Tax (7% of components)	$3,535	$3,850
Total	**$96,035**	**$138,850**

Table 7-5. Low and high bid proposal

ment, and installation costs.

The company liked both bids, but did not see the value of connecting the inventory system into the warehouse to be worth the cost of over $40,000. As a result, they chose the lower bid and Robert included that in his annual budget.

Presentation Formats

As we discussed above, a simple presentation might have just these elements:

- An agenda
- Photocopies of a one- or two-page budget for everyone at the meeting
- One page of either budgetary assumptions for an accounting-oriented meeting or notes on business value for a meeting focusing on departmental work
- Two copies of a few pages of supporting materials, available in case people ask additional questions

On the other hand, you may need to make a much fancier presentation with color graphics and a projector. These days, we often create a slideshow in PowerPoint or a similar computer program. The presentation may be displayed directly from a

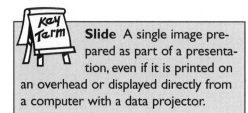

> **Slide** A single image prepared as part of a presentation, even if it is printed on an overhead or displayed directly from a computer with a data projector.

computer with a data projector or your company may use overhead projectors or even a slide projector. Find out what is available and make sure in advance that your presentation will work with whatever equipment you'll be using at the meeting.

The format of a presentation doesn't change the content. Prepare an agenda, a budget, and an outline of your talk. Once you know what you want to say and you have it organized, then you're ready to create a presentation. The easiest way to do this is to turn your outline into a set of slides.

Here are the steps of creating a good presentation:

1. Look at your agenda and decide how much of the time of the meeting will be spent on presentation and how much on introduction, discussion, and closure.
2. Plan on one slide for every two minutes of presentation. So, a 15-minute presentation should have only seven or eight slides. People need time to understand what they see.
3. Link your presentation to your agenda. Use agenda points as slide titles.
4. Highlight the most important points; don't cover every detail.
5. Most slides should have three to five bullet points. Never have more than seven.
6. If you can, include a few exciting or funny images.
7. Focus first on clarity and second on making it interesting.

Robert's boss, Svetlana, the Director of Information Technology, wants to present the value of IT to a meeting of the president and all senior executives in the company. She asks Robert to present the budget and to show that the company is getting good value for the money it's spending on IT.

Svetlana and Robert sit down to plan their presentations. Robert shows how he's organized the budget. Svetlana thinks it would be good to organize the presentation of the value of IT to match the parts of Robert's budget. They come up with these four main points.

- Keep the computers running!
- Everyone who needs a computer gets a computer!
- Save money through inventory control.
- Use efficient cost management.

Svetlana's presentation focuses on the value of each of these items, talking about effectiveness, synergy, and reduction of inventory losses. Robert prepares this outline for the talk he'll give with his 10-minute slideshow presentation of the budget and costs:

Keep the computers running!

- For only $30,000, we replace 20 old computers that are becoming unreliable. This routine replacement program reduces maintenance cost and downtime, increasing productivity.
- For only $6,000, we maintain an inventory of spare parts that allows for quick exchanges of failed equipment. This reduces lost work time.
- The annual maintenance program, costing a total of $42,125, is in its fourth year of operation. Costs per employee are going down each year because reliable, standardized computers are replacing the unreliable computers we used to have. With 180 employees using computers, the cost is only $234 per person.

Everyone who needs a computer gets a computer!

- HR checks with each department when a position opens to determine if using a computer is a job requirement. If so, they include that in the job description, include skill tests in the interview process, include computer training in orientation, and inform Robert that a new computer will be needed.
- Robert checks with HR to get the figure. This year, 10 new employees will get computers for a total cost of

$20,000.
- $15,000 for the basic computer
- $5,000 for special equipment (needed for certain jobs) and an increase to the spare parts inventory

Save money through inventory control.
- A basic system for this year
- Will cost under $100,000
- Should save $35,000 in inventory losses and lost orders per year
- Can be expanded to connect to the corporate network in the future

Use efficient cost management.
- Standard, modern equipment and standard training are saving us hundreds of thousands of dollars per year through employee effectiveness and efficiency. It keeps us ahead of the competition while costing us only $40,000 this year.
- The program to ensure everyone who needs a computer has a computer and is trained is reducing turnover, saving lots of money in HR for only $20,000 this year.
- The new inventory system will pay for itself in under three years.
- We avoided $40,000 in extra expense by keeping the inventory system simple and not linking it into the corporate network.
- We saved an additional $2,700 by planning ahead and consolidating computer purchases.

This is the shortened version of this outline that can be converted into a colorful slideshow:

Keep the computers running!
- Replacing computers: $30,000
  - reduce support cost
  - increase productivity
- Computer parts inventory: $6,000

- Total annual maintenance: $42,125
  - Fourth year
  - Cost per employee $234
  - Down from $260 last year

Everyone who needs a computer gets a computer!

- HR coordinates with departments
  - testing and training done by HR
- IT sets up computers before employee's first day
- 10 computers, $20,000
  - $15,000 for the basic computer
  - $5,000 for special equipment and spare parts

Save money through inventory control.

- Basic system under $100,000
- Saves $35,000 per year
  - reduce inventory losses
  - prevents lost orders

Use efficient cost management.

- People can do their jobs, not waste time with computer troubles. Saves hundreds of thousands, costs $40,000 this year.
- Everyone who needs a computer gets a computer, reducing HR costs by reducing turnover. Costs only $20,000.
- The new inventory system will pay for itself in under three years.
- Saved $40,000 by getting a simple inventory system that does the job.
- Saved $2,700 through consolidated purchasing.

Manager's Checklist for Chapter 7

- ❑ What are the parts of your budget?
- ❑ How would you plan each part, as production work or as a project?
- ❑ Can you build a consolidated budget for your department?

- ❑ Do you use account codes? If not, would they help?
- ❑ Do you have three sets of budgetary assumptions?
  - a detailed set for yourself, to make budgeting easier next year
  - a short one for accounting, focusing on financial issues
  - a one-page business summary of your budget
- ❑ Prepare an agenda for your next meeting and use it to run the meeting. See if it helps make the meeting less frustrating and more useful.
- ❑ Why are scope and level of detail important in preparing a presentation?
- ❑ Prepare yourself fully for a presentation using the seven steps to creating a good presentation. Then, don't forget to practice!
- ❑ Remember to create the content first—focusing on the purpose of the meeting. Making a presentation look good comes later.
- ❑ When could you use a presentation slideshow?

8

Budgetary Spending

What you want and what you get aren't always the same.

—Anonymous

The budget you create is more than an estimate of what you will spend; it is a request for permission to spend it. In this chapter, we'll look at how to get authorization for your budget and how to set up a spending plan for the year.

Getting the Budget Authorized

Sometimes, your budget is pre-authorized. The first time I had to make a budget, I was told that I had $50,000 to spend and it was my job to decide how to spend it to meet the goal of building a new computer network and running all the computers for a graduate school. There was no negotiation involved.

On the other hand, we often have to negotiate to get the money we need to do the work of our department. Many people think that negotiation implies big issues and major disagreements, such as unions fighting management and striking or

> **Pre-authorized** A budgetary amount that is defined and approved by the executive level before you prepare your department's budget.
>
> **Negotiation** Any process where two or more parties come together to make a decision.

governments making treaties. However, negotiation is a skill that we use every day, every time we try to reach an agreement with someone. As long as there are two or more people with different viewpoints, negotiation is the process of coming to an agreement.

There are four basic points you want to make in justifying your departmental or project budget:

- The value will exceed the cost. That is, the benefit of spending the money and doing the work is greater than the cost of the budget.
- The work plan fits within the company's long-term plans and does the work that the department or project is expected to do.
- You've made a good effort to reduce costs. That is, you're spending as little money as possible to get the work done well with quality materials.

You know what you're doing in running your department or project and preparing the budget.

Usually, making the first three points is enough to show that you know what you're doing. But there are some

> **Learn Negotiation from the Best**
>
> Negotiation methods that work for governments and major unions can work for you, as well. There's a wonderful book, *Getting to Yes*, by Roger Fisher and William Ury, from the Harvard Negotiation Project (Penguin USA, 1991). They have a good track record: They organized the Camp David accords that led to a peace treaty between Israel and Egypt. Their method is completely open: we don't hide anything. The approach works best if both sides adopt it.
>
> *Getting to Yes* can help companies make the best decisions about how to spend money to achieve corporate objectives.

extra steps that can help.

- Follow any management method or read books recommended by your company or your boss. If you use the company's approach and language, they will understand you more easily and accept that you know what you're doing.
- Understand management's concerns and focus. If you focus on quality and the finance department is focusing on cutting costs, you'll need to show how spending more money for quality equipment or parts now will reduce costs within the next year or, at most, three years.

As you meet with each executive or financial manager, listen to their concerns. If they want you to present first, present a basic outline and then ask for their questions or concerns. Listen, then respond to the particulars that concern the people you're meeting with.

Be Ready for Hardball

An IT manager for a major electronics manufacturer prepared a budget each year. He always tried to keep expense growth in line with corporate growth. If there was a 2% increase in staff size, he planned a support budget 2% larger than the previous year.

However, in this company, senior management was trained in hardball negotiation. Sellers would always demand more money and buyers would demand a cut in costs. They also used this method in the company, not just with their vendors. Every year, senior management cut back the numbers, refusing to grow the IT department budget. The manager had to manage a growing department on a fixed budget.

One year, corporate growth slowed and there were no plans to add new staff. The young manager went in and said, "Good news. I know you don't like to have the IT budget grow. This year, you can make it just the same as last year."

"Not good enough," the executive barked. "You should cut it by 5%!"

The young manager learned his lesson. If the company plays hardball, play hardball with them—he should ask for more whether he needed it or not so in the end he would get about what he requires.

In some companies, particular negotiation methods are part of the corporate culture or even part of the formal training for managers. Get any training and advice that you can so that you're prepared to present and defend your budget. For example, some companies assume that all departmental budgets are padded and automatically cut all of them by 10%. If you are new to management, you probably won't be able to change the system, so you'll have to go along with it. There are two different approaches to this, which we discuss later in "Block and Line Item Allocation."

Adjusting to the Authorized Amount

Senior management will approve your budget with or without adjustments.

If there are no adjustments, then you've got all of the money that you asked for. Your next step is to go to the accounting department with the approved budget. They'll enter it into the computer system and set up your accounts with the proper account codes and the amount you have authorized for each line item. We'll discuss this in detail below, under "Setting up Your Budget with Accounting."

If the budget has been adjusted, you have several choices:

- You can change your work plan or your project plan to fit the adjustments.
- You can look for alternative sources of money.
- You can request a meeting for reconsideration.

If you change your work plan, it's best not to cut each item by a certain percentage and just try to make things work. Some items, such as salary and purchases by contract, are fixed costs that you can't change. Instead, you should plan to reduce variable costs that are under your control. There are two ways to do this:

- Make a large cut in cost areas under your direct control to balance the whole budget.

- Change your work plan by eliminating specific activities and then revise the budget to reflect the fact that you are doing less work for less money.

Where can you go for alternative sources of money? That depends on your company. If you provide support within a company, you can turn to the departments you serve. They may have some discretionary funds. If you can convince those managers that their money is best spent on your project, they might chip in so that they can get the services they need from your department. If you work for a research organization, such as a university, you may be able to apply for a grant.

If the budget that came back to you seems impossible, then perform a gap analysis. If you use the reduced budget as best you can, what work will not be accomplished? What specific items do you need to buy and services do you need to acquire that you can't afford with the approved budget?

Lay out a clear picture of the problem, showing what you can do and what you can't do with the approved budget. Then take this to your boss. Walk through it with him or her. Your job is to show the consequences of different options and let the senior managers decide what they want to do.

Do not start by being either defensive or hostile. Simply present a choice to your boss or senior management:

- Here's what you asked me to do originally and here is what it would cost. (Show the original work plan and the original budget, revised downward a bit if possible.)
- Here's the revised budget and here's the work I won't be able to do if we have only the funds from the revised budget.
- Here's the difference in dollars.
- My question is this. If you want all the work done, can you come up with the necessary money so the department can do the work? If not, do you authorize the changes in the work plan?

At that point, you hope the people you are negotiating with

will find the money, approve the reduced work plan, or sit down and work with you to make the best choices. Take the approach of not blaming anyone, being reasonable, and being fair and see if they come along with you. If they do, great!

What do you do if they say, "No! Just make it work with what you've got and make sure you get all the work done." Clearly, they're not being reasonable. Still, there's no reason for you to become unreasonable. You might try this: "I'm going to do the best job anyone can managing this department and I'll deliver results for the company. I'd be happy to do an even better job. If you see how what you want is possible, then I must be missing something. Show it to me and I'll learn." At that point, they are most likely to sit down and work things out with you.

Some executives, however, never learn. Some companies have a dysfunctional corporate culture that keeps doing things in ways that just don't work. This discussion may just end with "Here's the budget; make it work." If so, don't despair. You're not the only manager in this company. Find another manager who is doing well. Take your colleague to lunch. Ask how he or she handles it. You may hear something like "Oh, it all blows over. In October, they run around and find extra money somewhere and things work out. This happens every year." Or, at another company, you may hear, "Well, just cut costs and do the best work you can. The productivity numbers don't matter much to the bean counters. But whatever you do, don't overspend your budget."

Please realize, we're not recommending these management approaches. But we want you to do the best job you can in your specific situation. If you stick with the program and do well, then you may gain influence over the years. Once you do, you'll be able to bring a more rational approach to your company's businesses methods of managing and budgetary planning.

Setting up Your Budget with Accounting

Accounting procedures vary a great deal. In this section we'll discuss some of the typical steps that occur when a budget is approved. The goal of these procedures is to set up the tracking system that will record expenses against the budget throughout the year.

Determining the Spending Period

Typically, budgets are annual. However, check with accounting to be sure. Make sure you know the start dates and end dates of the accounting year. Also, be aware of blackout periods when spending is not allowed. Some companies request that you not spend money in the last days of a month or quarter or year or at the beginning of a new year. They do this so that it will be easier to close the books for each period. In these cases, you're likely to see a memo that reads something like this: "All purchase orders must be submitted by December 20 to be included in this year's budget."

> Key Term
>
> **Blackout period** A period of time set by the accounting department or senior executives during which you may not make purchases or spend money for your department.
>
> **Closing the books** Work done by the accounting department to reconcile and check all accounts so that financial statements can be prepared. Typically, this is done every month, with some extra work each quarter, and a lot of extra work at the end of the year.

There may be additional restrictions about when you can spend money during the year. The accounting department may assume that you spend money steadily each month or each quarter. You may need to tell them otherwise, particularly if you're going to spend a lot of money early in the year.

To summarize, when you set up your budget with accounting, be sure to:

- Determine the beginning and end of the budget year.
- Find out about any blackout periods where you can't spend money. Then, place your purchase orders in time.
- Tell accounting about any unusual spending, especially higher spending early in the year.

Paying for Subscriptions

One situation that often creates a discrepancy between monthly spending and annual spending is subscriptions to professional magazines or journals. For example, Celeste totaled the subscription costs of the professional journals used in her department to be $1,440 per year. On her budget, that was annualized at $120 per month. However, all of the subscriptions came due for renewal in February and March. As a result, she needed to spend all $1,440 in the first quarter.

She saw this ahead of time. When she sat down with accounting, she told them she would spend the entire year's budget for that line item in the first quarter. Because they knew of the expenditure ahead of time, they adjusted the quarterly budget and there was no problem.

While you're working with accounting, have them review procedures for submitting purchase orders, getting payments approved and mailed, taking care of petty cash, and any other routine procedures.

Block and Line Item Allocation

Accounting is primarily concerned with control of the budget, that is, ensuring that the right people approve expenses and that spending does not exceed the budgeted amount. Working with your boss and the accounting department, you should define the level of authority you have in relation to your budget. There are two general questions about the authority that you should clarify:

- What parts of the budget do you have authority over?
- What limits or checks are there on that authority?

Typically, a manager will have authority over a budget in one of three ways:

- Expenses only, with no authority to change the amount allocated to each line item (a *line-item* budget). Using the example in Table 8-1, the manager would have authority over $41,000, but he would not be able to move money among the three categories: Printing, Utilities, and Telephone.

- Expenses only, with authority to reallocate line items as long as the total budget is not exceeded (a *block* budget). In this case, the manager of the marketing department would have control over $41,000 and could move money among the three categories or even spend it on other items, as long as the total expenses did not exceed $41,000.
- Expenses and salary, with authority to use each budget as you desire, but no authority to move money from expenses to salary or from salary to expenses. In this case, the manager would have control over $196,000. However, he could spend the $155,000 only on salaries and the $41,000 only on expenses.
  - This budget might operate as a block budget. In that case, the manager could change the salary structure on his own authority. He might hire a part-time account rep, pay him $15,000, and reduce support services to $15,000 by having all of the account reps do more of their own support work. He could also reallocate expense items.
  - This budget might operate as a line-item budget for expenses, for salary, or for both expenses and salary, in which case the manager could not move funds from one line to another without authorization.

Make sure that you know what parts of the budget you have authority over. Also make sure you know what you need to do if you plan to make changes to your budget. Even if you have the authority to move funds from one line to another, you may need to inform accounting in advance in order to do so.

If your organization works by giving line-item budgets, you may run into difficulty when the budget is adjusted. Most likely, the budgetary authorities will simply reduce every item by a percentage. Since some items are fixed costs, that simply won't work. You will then need to resubmit a budget with adjusted line items and the approved total and hope that they are willing to make the adjustments. If possible, request permission to do this

Marketing Department	2003
Expenses	
Printing	$20,000
Utilities	$20,000
Telephone	$1,000
Total Expenses	$41,000
Salaries	
Manager	$45,000
3 Account Reps	$75,000
Support Services	$35,000
Total Salaries	$155,000
Marketing Department Total	**$196,000**

Table 8-1. Sample departmental budget

in advance by saying, "If my department's budget is reduced below what I request, please allow me two weeks to submit a modified budget, adjusting the line items in the way that will allow us to get the most work done with the allocated budget."

Smart Managing

Delegating Budgetary Authority

When you give a team member the right to spend money, be sure you explain each of these points. Also, put them in writing:

- Why is this person empowered to spend money? Is it for convenience, to give him or her control of a job, or for some other reason?
- Which line items can this person spend from?
- What actions is this person allowed to perform? Spend petty cash? Authorize use of a charge card? Authorize a purchase order? Authorize a check? Others?
- Is there a dollar limit per expenditure or per month for this person?
- How will you see what spending has been authorized? How frequently? How quickly after money is spent?

Authorizing Your Team to Spend Money

In some accounting systems, the accounting department computer system tracks who approves each purchase order or check. You may want to approve each expense yourself or you may want to delegate authority to members of your team, to allow them to make certain purchases without checking each one with you.

Spending at the Beginning and the End of the Year

Several issues come up when we want to spend money at the beginning and the end of the fiscal year. One we already discussed is blackout periods—times when funds may not be available, even though they've been allocated. In addition, we need to pay attention to a few other factors:

- If the final budget approval is delayed, funds may not be available at the beginning of the year.
- In most companies, money not used by the end of the year is no longer available—it doesn't carry over into the next year.
- Although it's not a good business practice, many businesses figure that if you don't spend your entire budget within one year, then you'll need less money next year.

These fiscal policies can lead to a number of poor management practices. Departments may rush to spend money at the end of each fiscal year, either because the policy is use it or lose it or because they don't want next year's budget to be trimmed. These rush purchases are often unwise. Similarly, if accounting departments are unreliable in guaranteeing funding later in the year, departments may rush to spend early, even if that's not optimal for the workload and the management of work and money for the company.

These poor management practices are different from a genuine effort to handle a seasonal business that has ups and downs in available cash. It makes sense to schedule purchases

> **Budgetary Shenanigans**
>
> A long time ago, before I was a manager, I worked in the computer department of a public university. The position of director was not filled and several managers were working together to run the department. The prior director left before the budget was approved and it took several months to get a budget for the year. During those months, we had to request each expenditure as an allocation of emergency funding.
>
> Then, one day in September, the school administration approved the departmental budget. The next day, they announced that the school had run out of money for the year and there was a spending blackout for all departments for the year. The computer department got hit the worst because, without a director, it had no political clout.
>
> The goal of all of this was to save money. However, it ended up costing more money than it saved. The university did not approve renewal of the maintenance contract on the minicomputer that ran the entire school. When it crashed, it cost more to fix it just once than the entire maintenance contract would have cost.

when money is available, to reduce interest charges for credit or loans. These types of decisions are aimed at managing work in order to spend money in a wise way. But a decision to trim next year's budget because this year's budget was not fully spent falls into the error of thinking that last year's numbers are what next year's numbers should be.

Manager's Checklist for Chapter 8

- ❑ Is your department's budget preapproved? Or do you have to negotiate for the funds?
- ❑ Can you learn more about how negotiations work at your company? Is there anywhere else you could go to improve your negotiation skills?
- ❑ Write a plan to negotiate for your budget. Can you make a straightforward request? Do you need to pad the budget?
- ❑ Are you familiar with the accounting procedures you need to follow to set up a budget? To help close an accounting

period? To place a purchase order? To pay an invoice? To get a check cut? To handle petty cash?

- ❑ Do you have control of a block budget, or a line-item budget? If it's a line-item budget, what do you have to do to get money moved from one line to another?
- ❑ Are you responsible for salaries in your department? Do you think you should be?
- ❑ Is anyone on your team authorized to spend money from the budget? How do you manage and oversee those expenditures? Are you helping team members learn to take responsibility for managing the company's money?

9

Tracking Your Budget

He who has traveled ninety miles of a hundred-mile journey is best off thinking that he has gone only half the way.
—Chinese proverb

Creating our departmental budget and getting it approved is good work and good management, but it's really only the beginning. A budget is just a plan for how we'll spend money. During the year, we have to make sure that we're spending the money according to the plan. We also have to change the plan if we need to. We adjust the budget and request a change in allocated funds if plans change and we spend or need more or less than expected, so we can get our work done.

In this chapter, we'll discuss:

- Authorizing and tracking expenses
- Closing a budget period
- Comparing estimated various actual budgets
- Overspending and underspending
- Adjusting the budget
- Reviewing financial statements

Authorizing and Tracking Expenses

When the budget is approved and set up in accounting, we say that the money is allocated, but that it hasn't been spent yet. To track our expenses, we need to work at a more detailed level: we need to keep track of each purchase we approve and make.

> **Track** To track expenses means to make sure that we have good records for what we are spending and that we know how closely our spending matches our budget plan.
>
> **Adjust** To change a budget upward or downward during the budget year to adapt to changing circumstances.
>
> **Split** To allocate money from more than one line item to one purchase.

When we approve a purchase, we're authorizing spending money from a particular line item for that particular purchase. We make the purchase when we place a purchase order, use a business credit card, or use petty cash. At that moment, we should know which line item we're using for the expense. If we want to allocate money from more than one line item to one purchase, that's called a *split*.

Splitting a Single Expense

Suppose you're adding $500 to a postage meter. Rather than call this general office expense, you could estimate how much of the postage will be used for advertising, how much for shipping, and how much for general office mail. You might split the postage cost as $300 for marketing, $150 for shipping, and $50 as a general office expense. When you record the check to the post office, you create a split record in the accounting program, allocating money from three expense categories to pay one check. Table 9-1 illustrates the record of a split transaction. We say a transaction is balanced when the total debits (money taken out of accounts) equals the total credits (money added to accounts).

Using splits is an excellent way to keep a good budget. It lets you track expenses according to their purpose rather than just by items bought.

	Checking Acct.	Expense	Category
Debit	$500		
Credit		$300	Marketing
Credit		$150	Shipping
Credit		$50	General
Total	$500	$500	

Table 9-1. Splitting expenses

The Purchasing Process

A few years ago, almost all business purchase orders over $100 were arranged through approved purchase orders, with payment after delivery. Small purchase orders used a petty cash fund. However, with the advent of business credit cards and online ordering, a lot of business purchases are now by credit card. This is very convenient and it saves time. However, you can't allow a change in the way you send money to your vendors to open the door to poor accounting practices or poor budgetary tracking. You should be sure to allocate money from the appropriate expense line items each time you authorize a purchase. Trying to remember what a purchase was for later—at the end of the month, the quarter, or the year—leads to inaccurate records. And if our records are not accurate this year, we'll have difficulty planning next year.

When we track a budget, what we're really tracking, at a detailed level, is *transactions*. Each transaction moves money from one account to another within our budget. At the same time, each transaction is an agreement, sometimes a legal contract. Here are the transactions that occur with each purchase if we use a purchase order.

1. **Decision to buy.** This includes allocating funds from expense line items to the purchase and preparing a purchase order. It may include a contract with the vendor. In

the accounting system, money is allocated from the bank account to accounts payable.

2. **Receiving the item.** This includes either picking up the item or receiving a delivery or shipment. It also includes checking to make sure that the shipment is correct and that the items are not damaged. The packing list from the shipment is marked "received."
3. **Approving payment.** The packing list and invoice are brought together and checked. The account codes for the line item(s) are marked. The check can now be prepared.
4. **Making payment.** The check is prepared (often this is called *cutting the check*) and sent to the vendor. In the accounting records, money is moved from accounts payable to the appropriate expense category or categories.

If you pay by credit card, then the decision to buy also includes a transfer of funds from the expense account to the credit card account. Receiving and shipping are the same as with a purchase order. Payment is made to the credit card account rather than directly to the vendor.

Each day, you can identify the status of each purchase. If you add up all the current expenses, then you can find the status of each account for each line item. At any moment, the total amount you budgeted for the period equals the amount paid to vendors plus the amount committed by purchase decisions and the unused amount still available for future purchases. If you lose track of your purchases, then you won't be able to do this and you won't know how much money is still available to spend.

For example, let's say that we have a budget of $1,000 for the year for computer software. Earlier in the year, we spent $350. At the beginning of the month, we ordered one item for $100, and it has not arrived yet. We also went to a store and purchased an item for $75 on a credit card. The credit card bill has not yet arrived, but we have the receipt and we've approved the purchase.

The status of the computer software expense account is shown in Table 9-2. As you can see, the funds available for pur-

Budgeted	Spent	Committed	Available	Note
$1,000				Allocated for year
	$350			Spent in prior period
		$100		Hardware on order (Inv. # 124356)
		$75		Software purchase (credit card 7890)
			$475	Budgeted Less Spent + Committed

Table 9-2. Expense account status

chases for the remainder of the year equal the allocated funds less what has already been spent or committed.

When we commit to making an expense, we call that *accruing* the expense; and tracking expenses when commitments are made is *accrual accounting*, as mentioned in Chapter 2. If we track expenses only when we actually pay the money, that's *cash accounting*.

Businesses are much better off using accrual accounting. Otherwise, managers may overspend their budgets before they know they've committed to spend the money, especially when several people are allowed to charge expenses to the account. Each year, the accounting department prepares the figures for taxes and reports to the IRS based on either accrual accounting or cash accounting. But, whether the company reports to the IRS on a cash or accrual basis, you should track your department's income and expenses on an accrual basis.

Key Term

Cash basis Accounting system in which financial transactions are tracked when money is actually spent or received.

Accrual basis Accounting system in which financial transactions are tracked when commitments are made. Income is tracked when a client is billed and expenses are tracked when a purchase order is approved or a charge card is used.

Don't Accrue Income When the Contract Is Signed

It might seem reasonable to set up an accounts receivable schedule when a contract is signed. You expect to bill on a certain date and be paid on that date. But it's not a good idea. The contract might be cancelled or delayed for any number of reasons. You do not want to show income for work until the work is completed and the invoice is sent to the customer.

The proper way to track income projections from a contract is through your budget, under estimated income. You might want to divide estimated income into two categories: committed (for contracts or agreements signed by customers) and possible (for estimated sales and contracts or agreements under negotiation).

That means that you track your commitments to spend money, rather than only payments you make, and your contracts to earn money, rather than only payments you receive. When you sign a contract indicating that you'll do work and earn money, you accrue the income. When you complete the work and bill the client, you set up the money in accounts receivable. When the client pays and you deposit the check, you credit the income account with income received and credit your bank account with the money you deposit.

For example, suppose a consulting firm estimated that it would do work for three clients this month for a total of $300,000. One of the clients wanted one week of work at the beginning of the month for $80,000. That work is done and the client has been sent an invoice. A second client has signed a contract for two weeks of work at $150,000. The work is in progress and the client is not yet billed. The firm is negotiating with a third client, but there's no signed contract yet, so the firm can't count that in the committed part of estimated income. Table 9-3 illustrates the estimated income and accrued accounts receivable for consulting work for the month.

Estimated Income	Client 1	Client 2	Client 3	Total
Committed	$80,000	$158,000		$230,000
Possible			$70,000	$70,000
Total				**$300,000**
Accrued Income				
Accounts Receivable	$80,000	0	0	**$80,000**

Table 9-3. Estimated income and accrued accounts receivable

Closing a Budget Period

At the end of each period, whether it is a month, a quarter, or a year, the company needs to close the books. In a large firm, the accounting department does this; you help by making sure that they have all the information that they need. If you own a small company, you may do it yourself or you may work with your bookkeeper. The two most important bookkeeping jobs in closing a budget period are *balancing the accounts* and *reconciling the accounts.*

Balancing and Reconciling Accounts

Balancing the accounts, as defined in Chapter 2, means making sure that every transaction is recorded in two accounts—one where money is taken out (debited) and one where money is put in (credited). If the accounts do not balance, this means that we have lost track of some transactions, and we don't know where the money is.

The second bookkeeping job is reconciling accounts, as defined in Chapter 2. We reconcile all of the accounts that involve a transfer of money outside the company, such as checking accounts, credit card accounts, accounts receivable, and accounts payable. We do this for businesses the same way we do it for our checking account at home. We make sure that our internal records match the records from the bank or credit card company. When we reconcile accounts receivable, we compare our records to bills we sent out to our clients and checks we received from them. When we reconcile accounts payable, we compare our records to invoices we receive from clients and checks we sent out to them.

There are three important reasons why a business should close its books every month:

- If there are any missing records or errors, we catch and fix them while we still remember what we did.
- By reconciling accounts, we ensure that money is going where it's allocated. This makes it more difficult for anyone to embezzle—that is, to take money from the company illegally and hide the transactions by changing accounting records.
- Reconciling the accounts each month shows us what work we need to do to keep our business running well, as we discuss in the next section.

Follow-up Work

To run a business well, we need to do more than just know where our money is. We need to do work to get the money into the right place. First, let's look at some small jobs we can do while closing accounts, to keep the money moving through the company:

- **Billing.** We make sure that we've billed our clients for all completed work, increasing accounts receivable, an asset.
- **Collections.** We examine our accounts receivable aging record and do what we can to collect unpaid bills. An aging summary shows how much money is past due from customers. The aging detail report shows the customer and invoice numbers, allowing you to call or mail customers and ask for payment. The accounts receivable or collections department may do this or it may be part of your job to collect from the customers of your department.
- **Renewing petty cash and transferring money.** We add money to petty cash so we'll have enough for the next month. We make sure that we have enough money in the checking account by moving money from savings or, if

necessary, borrowing money from a line of credit.

- **Paying bills and loans.** We pay all bills, credit cards, loans, and lines of credit that are due or will be due before the end of the month so that we do not incur penalties, aggravate our vendors, or have unresolved items when we close our books.

When we have completed all the transactions we can and the accounting department has balanced the books and reconciled all accounts, then the books can be closed and a final version of the financial statements can be prepared.

Comparing Estimated Versus Actual Budgets

Once the books are closed for the period, we can create a spreadsheet that compares our estimated budget with our actual results. We can see an example for a single month in Table 9-4.

	January			
Expenses	**Projected**	**Actual**	**Difference**	**Variance**
Computer	$1,000	$850	($150)	-15%
Education	$250	$100	($150)	-60%
Insurance	$250	$250	—	0%
Marketing	$500	$500	—	0%
Medical	$1,500	$1,125	($375)	-25%
Miscellaneous	$250	$500	$250	100%
Office Rent	$450	$500	$50	11%
Office Supplies	$100	$50	($50)	-50%
Shipping & Post.	$50	$50	—	0%
Subscriptions	$100	$1,200	$1,100	1100%
Telephone	$100	$125	$25	25%
Travel	$250	$300	$50	20%
Total	**$4,800**	**$5,550**	**$750**	**16%**

Table 9-4. Estimated vs. actual for a single month

Overspending and Underspending

On each line item, we may be overspending or underspending compared with the estimate we made. So, we need to consider each variance in terms of the specific account and our circumstances.

Underspending slightly in January is probably fine, because it gives us more flexibility later in the year. For example, perhaps we underspent in Education because January is a busy time of year in our department and we plan most training for the summer. But if we find that we are underspending steadily for nine months, this could indicate that we are not following our work plan.

The overspending in Subscriptions seems like a big problem. But, when we take a look, we discover that we budgeted $1,200 for the year and all of the subscriptions came due in January. So, we spent the money early, but we are just fine for the year.

We're spending more than expected on Telephone costs. When we check into it, we discover that we've been asked to do more marketing and the expense is legitimate. We might look into requesting additional funds for the phone bill to meet the needs of the new marketing plan.

We get a clearer picture of how we're doing if we look at the actual vs. estimated expenses for an entire quarter, as in Table 9-5.

Here, we can see that there are no more subscription expenses, as expected. Telephone costs are doing well. We got the requested increase in projected expenses, but then we found a discount long distance service, so we're spending less. There's only one item of major concern: Medical. We look into it and discover that there was an end-of-year adjustment that saved us money, but the contract for employee medical insurance has increased from $1,500 per month to $2,000 per month. We'll need to request a variance to adjust for this.

If we have a block budget, then it's fine to decide to spend more on some items and less on others, as long as we do two things:

- We do not exceed our total budget for the period.
- We inform our boss and the accounting department of the change of allocation of funds in a timely fashion.

	January				February			
Expenses	**Proj**	**Act**	**Diff**	**Var**	**Proj**	**Act**	**Diff**	**Var**
Computer	1,000	850	(150)	-15%	1,200	1,300	100	-8%
Education	250	100	(150)	-60%	250	100	(150)	-60%
Insurance	250	250	—	0%	250	250	—	0%
Marketing	500	500	—	0%	1,000	750	(250)	-25%
Medical	1,500	1,125	(375)	-25%	1,500	2,000	500	33%
Miscellaneous	250	500	250	100%	300	100	(200)	-67%
Office Rent	450	500	50	11%	450	450	—	0%
Office Supplies	100	50	(50)	-50%	100	150	50	50%
Shipping & Post.	50	50	—	0%	75	75	—	0%
Subscriptions	100	1,200	1,100	1100%	100	—	(100)	-100%
Telephone	100	125	25	25%	150	100	(50	-33%
Travel	250	300	50	20%	100	100	—	0%
Total	**4,800**	**5,500**	**750**	**16%**	**5,475**	**5.375**	**(100)**	**-2%**

	March				Quarter			
Expenses	**Proj**	**Act**	**Diff**	**Var**	**Proj**	**Act**	**Diff**	**Var**
Computer	1,000	1,000	—	0%	3,200	3,150	(50)	-2%
Education	250	500	250	100%	750	700	(50)	-7%
Insurance	250	250	—	0%	750	750	—	0%
Marketing	1,500	1,350	(150)	-10%	3,000	2,600	(400)	-13%
Medical	500	1,500	2,000	400%	3,500	4,625	2,125	61%
Miscellaneous	150	75	(75)	-50%	700	675	(25)	-4%
Office Rent	450	450	—	0%	1,350	1,400	50	4%
Office Supplies	100	50	(50)	-50%	300	250	(50)	-17%
Shipping & Post.	100	50	(50)	-50%	225	175	(50)	-22%
Subscriptions	100	—	(100)	-100%	300	1,200	900	300%
Telephone	250	175	(75)	-30%	500	400	(100)	-20%
Travel	150	125	(25)	-17%	500	525	25	5%
Total	**4,800**	**5,525**	**1,725**	**36%**	**15,075**	**16,450**	**2,375**	**16%**

Table 9-5. Actual vs. estimated for a quarter

However, if we have a line-item budget and one or more items are overspent or underspent, then we need to request an adjustment. Similarly, if it looks like we need more money than we have in our total budget allocation, then we will need to request an adjustment to get the funds we need. We'll discuss this in the next section.

Adjusting the Budget

If the budget and actual amounts do not match, then it will be necessary to make an adjustment. The authority to do so may rest with you, your boss, or the accounting department.

Here are several different scenarios that will describe how you might adjust the budget.

1. If a single line item that's not under your control, such as a medical expense, has gone too high, you may simply explain the situation, write a memo, and get approval from your boss. The accounting department will adjust the allocated amount for the line item.

2. If you have a line-item budget and you're within your total spending limit, but some items are too high and others are too low, you should write a memo requesting an adjustment as early as possible. You may have to explain reasons for the variances. Organizations that have line-item budgets generally keep very close control and want explanations.

3. If you have a block budget but you believe you need to spend more money than allocated, you'll probably have to write a proposal explaining why the extra money is needed and what benefit the company will get from the additional expense. Be sure to state what work you will not be able to do if the budget is not approved.

4. If you're spending significantly less than you planned, discuss this with your boss and the accounting department as soon as possible. Otherwise, executive management may just assume you don't need as much money or that you overbudgeted and will cut your budget for next year.

Reviewing Financial Statements

Once all of this is done and the month is closed, we prepare financial statements for the end of the month. Based on these financial statements, we choose what business actions are best to keep the company going and improve its financial and business health.

Key Term

Asset Any item on a company's books that is part of the value of the company. If the balance sheet is prepared on an accrual basis, assets include accounts receivable.

Liability Any item on a company's books that reduces the value of the company. If the balance sheet is prepared on an accrual basis, liabilities include accounts payable. Liabilities are considered *short term* if they're due to be paid within the fiscal year and *long term* if they're due to be paid after the current fiscal year.

Equity The net value of a company, calculated as assets minus liabilities. The balance sheet shows how that value would be distributed to stockholders and owners.

Book value The value recorded on the accounting books for physical items, such as product or manufacturing inventory and equipment or property owned by the company.

Financial statements can be prepared for any time period. It's typical to prepare them monthly, quarterly, and for the fiscal year-to-date at the end of each month. The two most important documents in the set of financial statements are the balance sheet (Table 9-6) and the income and expense statement (Table 9-7).

The balance sheet shows the current value of the company as of any particular day. There are three major sections: Assets, Liabilities, and Equity. Here's the easiest way to understand the three terms: if the company settled all its accounts on this day, the assets would be its gross value (including money owed to the company), liabilities would be any money the company owes that would reduce its value, and equity (assets minus liabilities) would be the net worth of the company.

The income and expense statement shows how much money has come into and gone out of the company during a particular time period. In Table 9-7, we see the annual statement that goes with the balance sheet in Table 9-6. In this case, the owners do all the work; there's no payroll for staff to include under expenses.

When we look at the financial statements for any period, we can learn about the fiscal health and operational successes and

Balance Sheet as of December 31, 200x	
Assets	
Cash	$100,000
Accounts Receivable	25,000
Inventory	20,000
Total Current Assets	$145,000
Equipment	$250,000
Less Accumulated Depreciation	$150,000
Net Fixed Assets	$100,000
Total Assets	**$245,000**
Liabilities	
Accounts Payable	$50,000
Notes Payable	$50,000
Accruals	$25,000
Total Current Liabilities	$125,000
Long-Term Debt	$50,000
Total Long-Term Liabilities	$50,000
Total Liabilities	**$175,000**
Equity	
Common Stock	$50,000
Retained Earnings	$20,000
Total Equity	$70,000
Total Liabilities and Equity	**$245,000**

Table 9-6. A balance sheet

problems in the company. Here are some examples of conditions we might discover and actions we might take.

- **Getting new work.** If accounts receivable are low, we might want to focus on sales and marketing to increase work and accounts receivable.
- **Finishing work.** If we have contracts in place, but work is not yet done, then we can finish the work and bill it, so that we can move money from accounts receivable into our checking account.
- **Ordering materials.** If we have money available, but inventory is low, we can stock up on inventory or sup-

Income and Expenses, Jan 1–Dec 31, 200x	
Gross Sales **Cost of Goods Sold** **Net Sales**	$250,000 $150,000 $100,000
Expenses Rent Electricity Telephone Total Expenses	 $6,000 $3,600 $1,500 $11,100
Depreciation	$50,000
Total Expenses & Depreciation	$61,100
Earnings before Taxes	$38,900
Taxes	$15,560
Net Income	$23,340

Table 9-7. An income and expense statement

plies, looking for bulk discounts to reduce costs.

- **Resolving vendor problems.** If inventories are low or we've returned a significant number of items, that may indicate that our vendors are having trouble getting us what we need on time and with sufficient quality. We can address these issues with the vendors or look for new vendors.
- **Resolving customer account problems.** If our aging statement shows that some customers owe us money past due, we should discuss this with them. If this happens consistently, we may want to change our policy toward customers. For example, we can offer accounts to fewer customers and take credit cards for payment so that we get payment when services are delivered.

As you can see, closing the books and preparing financial statements are more than just bookkeeping chores. They allow us to check the pulse of our business so that we can plan our work.

Income All the money that comes into the company. Unless there are unusual sources of income (such as interest payments to the company), income is the result of sales.

Gross sales Total receipts from customers.

Cost of goods sold (COGS) The direct cost of purchased parts and materials included in items that are sold. COGS is most important in manufacturing and is linked to the change in the value of inventory.

Net sales Gross sales less COGS.

Depreciation An adjustment to the book value of assets owned by the company (such as equipment) that approximates the reduction in value of the asset due to aging.

Earnings before taxes Net sales less total expenses and depreciation.

Net income Earnings after taxes—the amount of money the company made in the period, increasing its equity.

Manager's Checklist for Chapter 9

- ❑ Do you have proper controls in place to ensure that all purchases are approved before they're made? Are the controls too tight, making it difficult for people to get what they need and get work done?
- ❑ Do you track transactions in a timely fashion? Or do you find that closing the month takes a lot of digging and too much guesswork?
- ❑ Do you keep your records up to date so that you can correct errors promptly and take care of work such as collecting overdue accounts receivable?
- ❑ Prepare an estimated vs. actual spreadsheet for one month for your department or have the accounting department do it for you. Then explain each variance and decide whether it's significant or not. For each significant variance, what action would you take to rectify it?
- ❑ Make sure you know the procedures for adjusting the budget at your company.

- ❑ Take a look at your company's financial statements for last year. If they're not available, look up the financial statements of any company's annual report. Walk through it and see if you understand it.

10

Budgeting and Human Resources

Companies manage payroll and human resources differently. Some organizations have corporate control of payroll and managers control only the expense budget. Others use departmental control, giving managers control over the human resource budget of their team. In recent years, the situation has been made more complicated by the use of long-term consultants to replace full-time staff. Money for these consulting services is an expense to the corporation, but the work is ongoing production work identical to what employees would do. Payroll and human resource management are handled by the vendor or subcontractor, not the corporation using the staff. This kind of contractor is often referred to as a "body shop," because it provides bodies—people to do the work—and the company that hires it manages the workers.

When companies use body shops, we end up with three major expense categories: payroll, general expenses, and consulting (body shop) services. The consulting services may be under corporate control or under departmental control. If con-

Human resources The business function that manages defining jobs, hiring and retaining staff, professional development, departure of employees, and payroll.

Payroll The business function that includes calculation and disbursement of paychecks and calculation, deposit, and preparation of payroll taxes and tax forms.

Body shop A vendor, contractor, or service provider that provides workers for companies, providing for their wages so companies can use workers for long term assignments without carrying them on the payroll.

sulting services are under departmental control, the manager may or may not have the authority to move money between consulting services and general expenses.

HR management The executive function of deciding how to organize staff positions and set general policy for human resource management.

HR services The routine work of managing payroll, job postings, and staff evaluation, development, and departure.

HR Management and HR Services

In order to understand how to manage and budget for human resources, we need to separate two parts of the job: HR management and HR services.

HR management includes:

- Deciding the organizational structure—that is, the staff positions within each organization and who reports to whom.
- Choosing applicants to hire.
- Making decisions on salaries and bonuses.
- Deciding for each position whether to use professional staff, staff on hourly wages, or a body shop.

Human resources services include:

- Calculating and paying routine payroll and payroll taxes, including annual salary increases.

- Managing hiring, including advertising openings, scheduling interviews, conducting HR department interviews, and employment-related testing.
- Managing professional development and employee retention and development policies.
- Managing employee reviews, terminations, and exit interviews.

Depending on the management structure, there are three ways of making the decisions involved in HR management:

- The senior executive level of the corporation may make all the decisions.
- The senior executive level of the corporation may make the strategic decisions, providing direction to HR, which develops policies.
- Departments may be more independent, having control of their own structures, job definitions, and salaries.

> Key Term
>
> **Departmental control** Accounting jargon for a business organization where each department controls its own payroll budget. HR services, such as payroll, are provided to each department by HR.
>
> **Central control** Accounting jargon for a business where the payroll budget is controlled and managed by HR or the senior corporate executives. Departmental budgets do not include payroll.

The first two methods above are called *central control* and the third is *departmental control.* Regardless of who makes the HR management decisions, HR services such as payroll are provided by the HR department.

Use of Consulting Services and Outsourcing

When companies do not want the cost of maintaining their own HR operations for permanent staff, they may use a body shop or outsourced services. In using a body shop, the company defines the job description and departmental organization. The vendor manages hiring and payroll, but the company manages the people as part of the department.

In using outsourced services, the company has the vendor provide the service and the vendor runs the department or team using its own management methods and structure, which may be different from those of the company that is hiring the outsourced service. The vendor provides the people and also manages them for the company.

This can be done in several ways:

- Particular departments may be outsourced. Commonly, companies outsource support services that are not directly related to the core business. Some common examples are the mailroom, maintenance staff, and computer support services.
- Body shops may be used to allow quick expansion and contraction of extra staff. A department may have a core staff of permanent employees supplemented by additional staff during peak seasons or times of high work demand. When demand drops, the outsourced staff are not retained, but they continue to work for their employer on other jobs.
- Outsourcing may be used for particular jobs, such as traveling sales or field representatives.

If you are moving to a new management position, be sure to find out who makes human resources, body shop, and outsourcing decisions. Find out if you are responsible for any HR-related responsibilities, including hiring, performance reporting, and job definition. This will determine the degree of departmental control—that is, how much control you, as a department manager, have over staffing decisions.

Departmental Control

If you have departmental control, then you will be making decisions about jobs, job definitions, and staff positions. Even so, you will not be responsible for the routine work of HR services.

The HR department will help you post jobs and conduct interviews. It will also take care of routine payroll and payroll tax responsibilities.

Staff Planning

If you have departmental control over HR resources, that means that you are given a block budget for staff salaries and you decide how it should be allocated. You can decide to have more people and pay each person less or to have fewer people and pay them more. However, you usually will not have the authority to transfer money between your staff budget and your expense budget.

In some cases, you may even have some degree of control over the total size of the department's HR budget. You can prepare a departmental staffing plan and budget, and then lobby to get the money that you need to get the work done.

You may decide not to reorganize your department at all. Perhaps you think that the current structure gets the job done well. If so, then you simply need to prepare a HR budget with the help of the HR department and accounting. If

Smart Managing

Incentives That Work

Here are some pointers for defining incentives that actually improve teamwork and results:

- Use half of the incentive money for incentives for the whole team when it meets departmental goals and half for incentives for each person.
- Develop clear, objective measurements of results and give incentives for goals that are achieved.
- Sit down with each team member and help him or her understand the key measure of productivity for the job. Then give an incentive based on that key measurement.
- Make sure that the measures for incentives are clear, fair, attainable, and understood by everyone.
- For incentives related to teamwork, let the team have some of the say in deciding who gets rewarded.
- Remember that incentives are not only about money. A hearty, public thank-you for work well done is greatly appreciated.

there's some extra money in that budget, you may want to develop an incentive program. Instead of either saving the money or raising salaries, you can define departmental goals and then reward the team and individuals for excellent work that helps the department and the company.

If you want to change job titles, responsibilities, and salaries, then you'll want to come up with a system that works. That is, you want to build a team that gets all of the work of your department done reliably and well. Of course, this is a very large topic, well beyond what we can cover in this book. But here's an approach that will get you started.

In planning departmental organization, think about it in two ways:

- Think about the work that needs to be done, independent of the people. Break it up into jobs. Who would do what and what would each person deliver? When each person delivers that item, who does it go to? You can use the seven steps to creating a work plan described in Chapter 5. Then ask who can fill the jobs you have defined and what positions you need to hire for.
- Think about the people on your team and what each of them can do best. Then, define the gaps. What work needs to be done that no one can do? Define jobs and hire people to do those tasks. Or, if those tasks are small, add them to the job descriptions of team members, explaining that everyone gets to do what they like most, but we also have to do some things that we don't like as much. We share the grunt work to get the job done.

If you have a new organizational plan supported by your team, you'll probably need to get it approved by senior management and HR. It's best to do this gradually. Even before you suggest changes, talk to your boss and other executives about the problem and about the need for change. Make sure that they are receptive to new ideas. Once they are, work with them and your team to build the ideas. That way, when the plan is

> **Don't Reorganize on Your Own**
>
> When making changes to job positions, don't do it alone. Get expert advice from senior managers and HR. They know a lot that you may not know. Even more important, work it out with your team. The best theoretical plan will become a disaster if your team doesn't understand it or resists the change. People often feel very insecure about changes in their jobs. You need to work with your team members, explain the need for change, include their ideas, and work together to come up with the best solution. When you have a good plan and the trust of your team, it's time to make the change.

complete, they'll already be on board, making approval an easier process.

Salary Planning

If you're responsible for the salary budget for your department, then you'll need to think about the best salaries and incentives for each job position on your team. There will be a number of factors to consider and not all of them are under your control. Here are the four most important points:

- *Do not overpay your employees.* When an employee is overpaid and then underperforms, this creates an extremely difficult situation. Even if the employee is unhappy on the job, he or she is unlikely to leave voluntarily if it means a pay cut. And there's little that you can do to create an incentive for someone who's already receiving a high salary.
- *Do not underpay your employees.* If you do, you create two problems. One is a revolving door where people do not stay very long. As a result, they never become very productive. As soon as they know their job, they leave for a place that will pay more. The second problem is that you will not get the best applicants to hire. You'll get people with poor skills or low self-esteem, who will not be as productive.
- *Use incentives effectively.* One solution that avoids the above problems is a moderately low base pay plus a gen-

erous but fair incentive program. Employees earn incentives based on the real, objective value of the work they do. That way, good performers earn and receive high salaries. Moderate performers earn reasonable salaries and know that they'll get more if they do better. Poor performers know that it's up to them to do better and to improve the results they deliver.

- *Be fair.* Even if salary information is supposedly private, word often gets around. If some people earn a lot more than others for the same job, for whatever reason, this is likely to lead to tension in the office. There are good reasons for differences in salary—more years of experience in the field or in the firm, more education, or a stronger work record. But be careful that the difference is not too large, that it has a good basis, and that those who make less money have a chance to take control of how they do their job and be rewarded for their efforts.

Once you have job descriptions for each position, you need to build a salary plan. This is a spreadsheet of salaries (annual or hourly) and work schedules. It is very important to get it right. An error here could lead to commitments and contracts that you can't easily back out of. And if those com-

For Example

Too Much Too Soon

The first time I was a manager, I had about a dozen student employees running a computer lab and I was responsible for hiring them and setting their salaries. When I started the job, it was summertime and, being very young, I was a bit panicked about getting good people. There weren't very many students around at all. One of them was excellent, but he already had another, high-paying student job. To get him to work extra hours with me, I needed to pay him $11 per hour. I did it, because I was afraid that I wouldn't get the lab started without help. When the semester started, I got other students, but the usual pay rate was only $6 per hour. The first student's extra skills were worth a higher salary, but the gap between $6 and $11 was really too large. It created some strain, especially when other student assistants learned their jobs and became excellent as well.

mitments put you over budget, then you'll have problems managing the department.

Each job position will be defined with a pay rate, usually an annual salary or an hourly wage. Before going any further, make sure that rules for work hours, holidays (standard and floating), vacations, sick days, overtime, comp time, flex time, and personal leave time are all clear. If not, you could end up with excess expenditures or with misunderstandings that lead to frustration and employee dissatisfaction. The business calendar and conversion spreadsheets from Chapter 3 will help you work this out.

Once the schedule and pay rates are clear, you will need to have the human resources or payroll department work out the payroll tax liabilities, benefits, and other deductions.

Key Term

Work hours The rules governing hours of work, including start time, end time, breaks, lunch, shifts, and days. Work hours are subject to corporate rules, union agreements, and labor laws.

Holidays Days that all or some employees in a company do not work, including legal holidays, extra days (such as the Friday after Thanksgiving), and floating holidays used to allow employees to choose when to take holidays.

Sick days Days that employees can take with pay due to personal or family illness. Usually, these are accrued and employees get a certain number of sick days per quarter or year worked.

Overtime Work hours beyond the normal for a work week. Usually tracked for employees with an hourly wage, and perhaps paid at time and a half.

Comp time Work hours beyond the normal for a work week. Sometimes tracked for professional, salaried employees, allowing them to take some time off to compensate.

Flex time Rules governing variations in start time, end time, and length of lunch break.

Leave Extended time off, paid or unpaid, for rare events such as a death in the family or the birth of a child. If unpaid, benefits continue and the employee is guaranteed a job when he or she returns.

Do not try to do this yourself. The rules are very complicated, they vary from state to state, they change frequently, and they vary with each worker's pay rate and number of family members. We're introducing the topic in this chapter only so that you can understand what payroll will do, not so that you can try to do it yourself.

Table 10-1 is an example of the information you might find on a basic pay stub. If an employee receives a weekly gross salary of $500 (that's $26,000 per year), then a simplified paycheck stub might look like what you see in Table 10-1. Although the employee earned $500.00, the paycheck is only for the net salary of $415.75. Where did the rest of the money go? To payroll taxes, including withholding for income tax and FICA (Federal Insurance Contributions Act), which comprises Social Security and Medicare. On most pay stubs, there would also be state deductions. In some areas, such as New York City, there might be local deductions as well.

Gross Salary	**$500.00**	
W-2 Withholding		$46.00
Medicare		$7.25
Social Security		$31.00
Total		$84.25
Net Salary	**$415.75**	

Table 10-1. Basic salary

In addition to what shows on the paycheck, the company also pays out money for each employee above the gross pay. The company matches the $38.25 (7.65%) FICA contribution for Social Security (6.2%) and Medicare (1.45%). (The company also pays unemployment insurance—FUTA, Federal Unemployment Tax Act—for each employee.) Above a certain salary, currently $84,900, nothing is withheld for Social Security, but the Medicare rate of 1.45% continues to apply. (These figures are adjusted from time to time.)

The basic salary in Table 10-1 is just the beginning. There

are several other items that might be added to a paycheck. The general categories are listed here:

- **Pre-tax withholding.** Certain benefits, such as retirement plans and some health insurance, can be taken out of the paycheck and paid directly to retirement accounts or insurance before taxes are deducted. The employee gets a smaller paycheck, but also pays less tax each year and gets the additional benefit.
- **After-tax withholding.** Some additional amounts may be withheld after tax deductions, because the money is being sent to a special account, but it is taxable. Union dues and charitable contributions might be examples.
- **Additional taxes.** The federal tax amount will vary depending on the employee's exemptions based on the number of dependents (family size and other factors). State and local taxes may apply. Unemployment insurance (FUTA—Federal Unemployment Tax Act) will usually be withheld, but this is paid by the employer, not by the employee.
- **Bonuses, commissions, variable hours, and overtime.** These items might change the gross pay on a paycheck. Since tax rates vary with the pay rate, they can also change the withholding amount and even the withholding percentages.

Table 10-2 illustrates one of these items, a pre-tax deduction for insurance. The employee pays for the insurance, so it's deducted from his or her pay. But it's a tax-free benefit, so it's deducted before taxes are calculated. Taxes are calculated on only $465, instead of $500, reducing the amount of taxes withheld.

Table 10-3 shows what the last check of the year for the same employee might look like if the employee received a $5,000 bonus. This shows why it's important to explain payroll and deductions to your team members. Imagine how an employee will feel if he or she is expecting a $5,000 bonus and then gets a check for only $4,573.25!

Salary		
Gross Salary	$500.00	
Benefits		
Pre-tax Insurance		$35.00
Taxable Income	$465.00	
Deductions		
W-2 Withholding		$41.00
Medicare		$6.74
Social Security		$28.83
Total Deductions	$76.57	
Net Salary	**$388.43**	

Table 10-2 Basic salary

Salary		
Gross Salary	$500.00	
W-2 Withholding		$46.00
Medicare		$7.25
Social Security		$31.00
Total Deductions	$84.25	
Net Weekly Salary	$415.75	
Bonus		
Bonus	$5,000.00	
W-2 Withholding		$460.00
Medicare		$72.50
Social Security		$310.00
Total Deductions	$842.50	
Net Bonus	$4,157.50	
Check Amount	**$4,573.25**	

Table 10-3 Basic salary

It's important to remember that some incentives—such as some types of insurance, transportation costs, and support for

The Negative Paycheck

If you manage a restaurant, you may want to tell your employees about the possibility of a "negative paycheck." Otherwise, some employees may get a rude surprise when they see their paychecks—the stub may indicate that they owe money to their employer!

Restaurants are required to withhold taxes for an employee's tips as well as his or her hourly rate. Many employees take their tips home as cash. If the salary is low and the tips are high, the paycheck may end up having more withholding than there is pay! The result is a pay stub and no check—and the employee has to pay the restaurant money to make up for what was sent to Uncle Sam!

relocation (moving expenses)—are counted as additional taxable salary, increasing the deductions on paychecks.

Putting It All Together

After you've created a spreadsheet showing salaries and rates for each employee, you should give it to HR and have them add withholding information. Then build a single budget spreadsheet showing the department's total HR budget—all salaries and wages for all staff. Make sure to note whether or not the total includes the corporate liability for extras such as the corporate contribution to Social Security and any employee benefits above salary that do not appear on the paycheck, such as employer contributions to health plans, insurance, or perks such as health club memberships.

Review the spreadsheet carefully with HR, accounting, and your boss. Check for items that might change, such as midyear raises. If employees are unionized or have employment contracts, make sure to check your figures against all appropriate guidelines, agreements, and contracts. The result will be your department's HR budget for the year.

After the budget closes for the fiscal year, HR and accounting will be able to generate an actual vs. estimated spreadsheet for salary and human resources costs for the year. Since most salary figures are preplanned, there will usually be very little variance. However, three things can lead to major variances:

- **Unfilled positions.** If a job was vacant for a period of time, then less money was spent than budgeted.
- **New hires at higher or lower cost.** When you fill a position, you may find that you need to pay more than you expected. You may be offering a higher salary to get a good person, a one-time payment to support relocation, or a bonus to the employee who recommended this person. Or, in some cases, a new employee may cost less than expected.
- **Changes in benefits and benefit packages.** Changes in benefits, especially medical plans, are common these days. You need to identify what those changes are and how they affect your HR budget.

In looking at a variance report for HR, be sure to check whether the difference between estimated and actual is the result of one-time events (such as an unfilled position or a relocation bonus) or permanent changes that will affect future budgets (such as a higher salary for a position or a change in benefits). That will help you plan next year's HR budget.

Manager's Checklist for Chapter 10

❑ Who makes HR decisions for your team? Do you have departmental control?

❑ Do you use a body shop or outsourced services? If so, do you manage the budget for that service? If not you, then who?

❑ Do you need to be able to lobby for changes to the HR budget or the budget for consulting, body shop, or outsourced services?

❑ Can you explain your pay stub? Can you explain the pay stub of everyone on your team? If you have some professional staff and some union employees, can you explain both types of pay stubs?

- ❑ What benefits add to the company's cost per employee above gross pay?
- ❑ What benefits are taken out of an employee's pay before taxes, reducing tax withholding?
- ❑ What would you do to prepare for a salary negotiation when hiring a new employee?
- ❑ During a job interview, after you've offered a salary, a prospective employee asks what her take-home pay will be. How would you answer her question?

11

Small Business Money Management

Some would rather be a big fish in a small pond than a small fish in a big pond.

—folk saying

Many managers who have run departments think they're ready to go out on their own and launch a business. 10 years ago, I thought so. And I did—I launched a business and it's done very well for 10 years. But, looking back, I would say that I've had to learn an awful lot about budgeting and about management to be able to do it. Eight out of 10 new businesses fail in the first three years; good money management and budgeting skills are crucial to success. So, if you've understood everything in this book so far and you think you are ready—read on. I'll share what I've learned in the last 10 years to make your road a bit easier.

Every new business—in fact, every business—needs a business plan. Many people think that a business plan is used mostly to get investors—venture capitalists—to give you money. Actually, that's not the most important function of a business

A Business Is More than Money

As a consultant, I've reviewed many business plans. Some set goals of serving customers better, serving more people, or offering a new and valuable product that will improve people's lives or make business easier. Other business plans, however, focus just on money: "increase revenue by 50% in three years" or "cut expenses and increase net revenue by 30% this year."

In my view, purely financial plans are not good business plans. Businesses do make money, but not if that's their main purpose. Money is a side effect of serving our customers. When we do good things for our customers, we count the money as the measure of our success.

plan. A business plan should be a plan for your business. What will you offer your customers? What are your goals? How will you make money? How will you spend money? How will you grow?

The business plan should be a guide for your business. It should define the services you offer your customers and the benefits of those services. It should define the work you will do and the people who will do it. At the most detailed level, it should define benchmarks—the key measures that determine if the business is in good shape. Is enough work coming in? Is enough money coming in? Are expenses as low as you expected? Do you have the inventory you need? We define those num-

Don't Believe Your Own Numbers

When we write a business plan, we're excited about what we hope to do. And a business plan is a marketing tool: we want to get others, especially investors, excited as well. All of that is well and good, but it can lead to inflated estimates of income and unrealistically low estimates of how much time and money it will take to get the business started.

When you build a business plan, plan for the worst as well as the best. Don't get caught up in the mistake of being certain that everything will go great and the business will grow without problems. It may look that way on paper—or in a four-color presentation—but, if you want your business to succeed, you need to have a plan that allows for things to take longer, cost more, and be more complicated than you would expect.

Smart Managing

Learn from the Best

There are many good books on writing business plans. My own favorite is *Business Plans That Win $$$: Lessons from the MIT Enterprise Forum* by Stanley R. Rich and David E. Gumpert (HarperCollins, 1987). The MIT business forum allows entrepreneurs to present their business plans to venture capitalists, who then critique the plans and give advice for making a good business plan, getting venture capital, and succeeding. My favorite part of the book is where it asks probing questions that help you understand your reasons for starting a business so that you can decide if it is really right for you. Starting a business takes all that you have to give, and the more you know going in, the better.

bers in the business plan, and then we track the progress of the business by comparing actual figures with the business plan.

Estimating Business Income

Creating a realistic, accurate estimate of business income is the biggest challenge of setting up a business plan. It is easy to think, "I'll work 40 hours a week, charge $100 an hour, and work 50 weeks a year. That's $200,000 a year." It may be easy, but it's also completely unrealistic.

First of all, when estimating income, you don't estimate how much work you will do. Instead, you have to estimate how much money other people will pay for the work you do—or for the things you will sell. Second, if you work 40 hours a week for pay, when will you find time to run your business, do marketing and sales, and take care of problems? You might think that you can just hire other people to run the office for you, but that just doesn't work. Managing people takes time, especially in a small business. When I bring employees into my company, I tell them that I want them to reach the point where they can work 10 hours for every hour that they spend with me. But very few employees are able to be that independent, that flexible, and that self-directed. Usually, you end up spending an hour with each employee for every four hours they work—and that's when there are no problems.

How do you estimate how much money other people will pay for your products or services? Here are some tips:

- Calculate each product or service separately.
- Think about your customers: Are they businesses or consumers? Who will make the buying decision? How much money do they have? How much would they spend to get whatever you offer from someone else? What advantages do you offer? Is your product or service less expensive, more convenient, or better? If it's not less expensive, why will people choose to buy it?
- Pretend to be one of your customers. Be realistic. If you build a business on the idea that people will want you to wash their car every week, you won't succeed. You have to offer real value for real success.
- How many customers will you have? Where will they be?
- How much will they buy?
- How often will they come back?
- What would cause a customer to buy more, to buy less or stop altogether? Which of those elements are under your control? More important, which ones are not?
- How long will it take to build a customer base?

Once you see your business from the customer's perspective, you can develop a marketing and sales plan. From a budgeting perspective, you've started to estimate how much income you will have. It's a very good idea to do a low, medium, and high estimate of projected income for each product or service.

If you can deliver everything your customers want, then your marketing plan drives your business plan. But that may not be the case. There may be some other limiting factor, often called a bottleneck. If you can't produce as much as you can sell, then the limiting factor is in production—and it will limit your income, because you can sell only as much as you can produce. Here are some examples of limiting factors:

- **Production capacity.** If you have a factory, you can sell only as much as you can manufacture.

- **Supplies.** If you import rare or specialized items, you can sell only what you can find and buy.
- **Delivery.** You can sell only what you can deliver. Pizza places often lose sales on rainy nights. They could make all the pizzas that people order, but they can't get them all delivered.
- **Logistics.** This is a fancy word for the coordination of getting supplies, putting things together, and delivering the product or service. Whatever the bottleneck is in the production and delivery, that's the limit on how much you can sell and how much money you can make.
- **Expertise.** Some jobs require experts that may be hard to find and expensive to retain. In those cases, the limiting factor is either retaining the expertise or the cost of that expertise.

When you understand the bottleneck in your business—and there always is one—then you can estimate your business income.

The next step in a business plan is to define business operations: what work will be done, by what departments, with what people? This will lead to your estimate of expenses. Then you'll need to define how you'll acquire raw materials and supplies. This will lead to your cost of goods sold budget. You should be able to project minimum, likely, and maximum financial statements for the first two or three years of business.

This is obviously a very brief introduction to creating a business plan. Take the time to read, study, think, revise, and make the plan as good as you can. Your financial projections should be a result of the products and services you plan to offer and the work you plan to do. Remember: numbers don't create numbers. A good budget is the result of a good work plan.

So, now let's turn our attention to the details of a small business financial plan. We'll focus on the most difficult parts of the financial plan and those parts that are different from general management. So, if you're planning to start your own business, make sure you use all the methods and tips in this book, not just the ones in this chapter.

Small Business Payroll

In planning human resources for a small business, read Chapter 10 carefully. It's easy to imagine a bunch of dedicated, flexible workers who care as much about your dream as you do. And, if you're excited about your business, employees will probably be inspired when you interview them. Ultimately, though, your dream is not their dream—it's just their job. They will expect more stability than you may be able to provide and may be less dedicated than you expect.

If you decide to offer flexible hours or benefits and goal-oriented incentives, make sure that you hire people who appreciate these alternatives and will respond well to incentives. Also make sure that you design an incentive program you'll be able to afford no matter how poorly—or how well—your business is doing.

Human resources management for a small business is best delegated to a professional service. Small companies are too small to have their own HR departments. Generally, you'll want to consider two services—a benefits service and a payroll service.

In planning employee benefits, you may simply want to find a company that offers prepackaged plans and services, or you may want to work with a small business financial advisor to set up health, retirement, incentive, and benefits plans.

For payroll, it's best to get a professional payroll service. Payroll deposits, which may need to be made weekly or monthly, and payroll tax reports are very complicated and the rules change often. The federal government monitors payroll deposits, payroll reports, and payroll tax forms very closely. It takes any errors very seriously and they're difficult to correct. You do not want to have a crucial business relationship with the Internal Revenue Service depend on one employee who may make a mistake, get ill on the day the payroll deposit is due, or leave the company unexpectedly. In addition, the IRS knows that professional payroll services such as Automated Data Processing (ADP) and Paychex do the job right and spend less time scrutinizing your payroll for errors.

CAUTION!

Use a Payroll Service and Never Miss a Payment

It's important to use a payroll service to avoid mistakes and problems that can lead to excessive interest, penalties, and time-consuming bureaucratic hassles. It's even more important to always make payroll taxes on time—usually the same day you cut paychecks. When money is tight, it may seem tempting to pay your employees on time and pay the government their payroll tax deposit (for withholding) a bit later. However, this is a federal offense that has a good chance of landing you in jail.

General Financial Management

The time you spend managing money is time you don't spend making money. Every company, no matter how small, needs work done for billing, accounts receivable, accounts payable, and general bookkeeping. Most need timesheets as well. It may add up to only a few hours a week, but it's crucial that you not fall behind. Being up to date in bookkeeping and financial management has these advantages:

- You reduce the cost of late fees, penalties, and interest.
- You see problems coming, because you catch them sooner.
- You get a better feel for your business because you know how the money is coming in, where it is going out, and how much you have.
- Your records are more accurate, because they're not based on inaccurate memories of what might have happened.
- Being on top of the business and having clear records makes planning and forecasting much easier.

The problem is finding enough time to keep up to date on the bookkeeping. Each small business owner needs to decide whether to do it himself or herself or to hire a bookkeeper or use a bookkeeping service. Whichever you do, I recommend that you know enough to be able to do it yourself. That way, you can

Time, Money, and Peace of Mind

Many small business owners try to avoid spending money. Being careful about money is important, but it's not the only issue. When we choose not to spend money, we need to do the work ourselves. But, having free time to solve problems and grow the business is essential. So, it may be better to hire help to do routine work. It's easier to find reliable bookkeepers and accountants than to find specialists in your business area. So, it makes sense to hire help for financial management.

There's one other issue that affects some business owners—stress. If we become too stressed, we lose time for work. Even if we don't actually get sick, we have a hard time focusing and thinking clearly. If having a professional take care of the books will help you relax and stop worrying about keeping track of the money or about finding the time to pay the bills, then that money to hire professional support is well spent.

tell if your bookkeeper is doing a good job. Also, you can evaluate the books and do a better job planning your business.

If you want to save both time and money, plan to meet with your accountant at least once a year. Have the accountant review your budget and account codes. He or she may recommend using different account categories that will save you money on taxes or may make other suggestions. Also, go over your financial statements for the past year along with your taxes so that you understand them thoroughly.

Seasonal Fluctuation and Available Cash

Companies have ups and downs, and some of them are predictable. If you are in a seasonal business, then be sure to plan ways of having enough money to get through the low periods. There are several options to consider:

- **A line of credit.** This is a revolving loan. You can borrow whatever you need up to the maximum of the credit line, you pay interest only on what you borrow, and you can pay it back as soon as you have the money, even if you need to borrow it again the next month. Classically, lines of credit were easy to get if they were backed by accounts receivable. There was good reason for this: if your company runs into trouble or closes, the bank can take over the accounts payable and collect the money without trying to run your business. In the last few years, with more customers paying by credit card, accounts receivable is much lower, so it's harder to get large lines of credit.

- **A loan.** If you have a record of good sales and high net revenue during your busy season or if you have some asset (such as a building) to use as collateral, you can get a loan that will get you through the lows.
- **Investing in your own business.** If you have enough extra money, it can make sense to invest money in your own business. However, it's a very bad idea to use up your own savings or put up your house or other essential personal assets to support your business. It's good to have confidence in yourself, but it's not good to put all your eggs into one basket.
- **Having friends invest.** This is generally not a good idea, if you want to keep your friends. Remember that 80% of small businesses go under in the first three years. If you close the business and can't pay them back, you will lose a lot more than money. If banks or investors wouldn't give you money, why would you ask friends to take the risk? Friends and family who invest not expecting much chance of return are often called *angels*.
- **Venture capital.** Venture capitalists are people who make a business of investing in new businesses. They know the risks and they are looking for a high return. Small businesses are often too small to interest them. In addition, there's a chance that you will lose control of the business if you can't deliver the rate of return the investors expect.
- **Stock offerings.** If you are ambitious, you might look into an IPO (initial public offering). This offers the public stock in your business. Regulations are complicated, but there are some interesting alternative choices that can simplify the process, such as offering stock only within your home state.

As a general rule, you want to plan to have enough money to run your business with room to spare. Otherwise, you may find yourself relying on credit card debt, which is very expensive due to high interest rates. As a small business owner, you will almost certainly have to cosign any loan to your business.

One of the worst things that can happen to a small business owner is that the business fails and then the debt of the business becomes personal debt. Even if you can return to the world of regular paychecks quickly and with a high salary, it will take a good deal of time to pay off those debts. As much as possible, ensure your own personal financial security and don't allow your enthusiasm and love for your business to jeopardize your personal life.

Managing Accounts Payable When Money Is Tight

In the routine operation of your business, there will be times when it's difficult to pay the bills. You should have a plan for these situations before they arise. Here are some options. You should make a prioritized list of your own similar to this one:

- Borrow money from a line of credit or get a loan.
- Make partial payment on bills from major suppliers. Don't just send the payment. Call their accounts receivable department, explain the situation, and set up a payment plan. Follow up the call in writing with a statement that you can refer to. That way, if a vendor cuts off supply, you can refer to the letter and maintain a good relationship.
- Make arrangements for extended payment terms, such as paying in 60 or 90 days instead of 30.
- Work out arrangements with your staff for delaying paying them.

Of course, you hope you never have to do the more difficult tasks listed further down. But it's better to think of them in advance and even sound out your vendors and staff on what they are willing to accept. This will make it easier if hard times do come.

I prefer an approach called *honest business* or the *open book approach*. There are many ways of delaying making payments by hiding things, such as saying the check is in the mail or your bookkeeper is ill. Instead, I prefer to be straightforward about problems and solutions. I find that, when I am, most people want me to succeed and are willing to work with me for a good solution. A good vendor knows that allowing a delayed payment now earns my loyalty later when my business grows and I want to buy more. Consider running your business in such a way that if everyone knew all the details, no one would have any complaints.

Setting Prices

Marketing meets budgeting when we set prices for what we sell. Setting prices is complicated; it's important to look at possible prices from four perspectives:

- **The buyer's perspective.** If the price is too high, then it will not be worth the cost to the buyer. Make an effort to determine the hard dollar value of what you sell to your buyers.
- **Your own company's perspective.** If you sell for too little, then you will lose money, even if sales are high.
- **Your competitors' perspective.** If you charge more than your competitors, then why should anyone buy from you? If you charge the same, how will you distinguish yourself? And, if you charge less, will they cut price to match your price, creating a price war where no one makes any money at all?
- **The market perspective.** It is good to understand the relationship of supply, demand, and price. It's hard to predict how prices will change in the future, but you should put some thought into it.

Budgets for Customer Proposals

Sales meets budgeting when we prepare proposals for our customers. In some businesses, we don't set prices or we don't pub-

The Price of Live Fish

For Example

Many years ago, my father and I went on vacation. We went skin diving with a tour guide who made his living collecting rare fish and sea animals and selling them to people who had saltwater aquariums. He told us that business was always slow during the summer. My father, who is an economist, pointed out that during the summer, people like to go to the shore themselves and do their own collecting. The problem wasn't that fewer people were putting things in their aquariums during the summer; it was that people were collecting things for themselves. Once the sea collector understood where his competition was, he could adjust his business. For example, he could offer to take his customers to go skin diving and do their own collecting.

lish them. Instead, we do custom work and we prepare a proposal for each job. The price we propose must be low enough that the customer will consider hiring us and high enough that we will make money if we take the job. In addition, if our proposal is a competitive bid, then our price must compete with the prices of bids from the other vendors that the customer is considering.

Flexible Pricing

Smart Managing

It would be a mistake to set a price and then print thousands of price tags and expect the price not to change for a year. When you advertise, you can advertise a price as being "for a limited time only." If you sell more than you produce, raise your price. If you don't sell enough, offer a sale and then, eventually, lower your price. Ultimately, the only way to learn the best price is to try a price and see what happens. You know you've got the right price when you sell what you've got, but you couldn't sell any more.

Table 11-1 illustrates one way of thinking through a bid. In this case, my company was asked to act as a body shop, providing technical staff to complete computer installations. Our customer would charge their customers either $125 or $150, depending on the contract with the customer. They would retain 35% and pass the rest on to my company. My company would retain 40% of what it received and pass the rest on to the workers. We prepared Table 11-1 to illustrate whether this was worth doing.

A	B	C	D	E	F	G	H
	Customer retains		Vendor receives	Vendor retains		Vendor pays staff	
Hourly rate customer charges clients	Percent	Dollars	Dollars	Percent	Dollars	Dollars per hour	Dollars per week
$125	35%	$43.75	$81.25	40%	$32.50	$48.75	$1,950
$150	35%	$52.50	$97.50	40%	$39.00	$58.50	$2,340

Table 11-1. Calculating bid profit and expenses

My company is the vendor, so the important column for me to evaluate is Column F, the money I will retain for work done. My staff looks at columns G and H to see how much they will make per hour and per week. If my staff and I are satisfied with what we will receive, then the bid is worth it to us. If the customer is willing to accept the value in Column C, then they will be open to accepting my company's bid.

There are different types of competitive bids. Sometimes, either by law or by the customer's policy, the lowest bid is the one that will be taken. Other times, all bids will be considered and the one that offers the highest value for cost will be taken, even if it doesn't have the lowest price tag. What would make a customer consider a bid that's not the lowest cost?

- **Proven reliability.** If the customer is more confident that you can deliver the service than that the lowest bidder can, the customer may prefer your proposal, even at higher cost.
- **Higher quality.** If you can show that you add some quality—a more reliable product, better customization, better training, or something similar—then your proposal is more likely to be accepted.
- **Added value.** Some specific item that you include in your proposal that benefits the customer's company may make the higher price worthwhile.

When you write a proposal and a bid, make sure the two fit

Know Your Customer's Approach

When preparing a bid, you want to know the ground rules and the customer's concerns. Most customers will be glad to answer your questions in advance—it helps them get a better proposal. Be sure to ask these questions:

- Will the lowest-cost bid be chosen? If not, what are the criteria?
- Who will make the decision?
- What are that person's and the company's biggest concerns about the job—time, cost, quality, reliability? Please be specific.
- Is there a format for the proposal? If not, what material is available?
- What is the timetable? Will there be a process of discussion and bid revision? A process of negotiation? What date will the choice be made? When will the job start?

well together. Here are some things you can do to make a clear bid proposal:

- Make a numbered list of the products and services and features you will provide. Include a line-item budget that matches those products, services and features.
- Make a clear statement about all expenses, such as travel, per-diem rates, or items you purchase for the client. If you know the exact cost when writing the bid, include it. If not, make a two-part bid proposal, one part with fixed costs and a subtotal, and another part with estimates of variable costs and a subtotal.
- If you're offering special rates or a discount, make sure you put that in writing and also include it in the budget.
- Be sure to include a date past which the bid is no longer valid. If the customer does not decide by that date, you may change the price.

For example, if a client asked my company for a two-day seminar plus a day of consulting about their organizational structure, this would be an excerpt from my proposal:

Two-day advanced management seminar for 15 executives, $8,000. This seminar will provide executives everything they need to oversee departmental budgets, save money, and increase productivity.

Strategic planning meeting. A meeting with senior management based on a prepared agenda. We will identify the company's strengths and weaknesses and also the opportunities and threats the company faces due to technological change and competition in the marketplace.

Preparation of agenda. Six hours of telephone meetings and preparatory work for the consulting services.

Report and recommendations. A complete, written report of all issues, decisions, and recommendations based on the strategic planning meeting.

Travel arrangements will be made by the client.

This proposal would include Table 11-2. Note how each line in the proposal matches a line in the budget and how the budget presents the bid proposal cost to be paid to the vendor ($17,400) as well as the total cost, including expenses handled directly by the customer ($19,350). Over the years, I have found that clients deeply appreciate this straightforward approach with no hidden costs.

Manager's Checklist for Chapter 11

- ❑ Have you ever thought that starting your own business would be easy? Does this book make you rethink that?
- ❑ Could you start your business without risking your personal income or savings?
- ❑ Do you have a plan for your business?
- ❑ Think about three people you know who could read your plan and help make it better.
- ❑ Can you think of an example where someone believed his or her own marketing hype? What happened?
- ❑ Does your business have seasonal fluctuations? If so, where do you get money to handle the slow periods?

Item #	Item	Rate	Time	Total
1	Advanced management seminar	$4,000/day	2 days	$8,000
2	Strategic planning meeting	$4,000/day	1 day	$4,000
3	Agenda preparation	$300/hour	6 hours	$1,800
4	Report and recommendations	$300/hour	12 hours	$3,600
	Total payable to vendor			**$17,400**
5	Travel expenses (estimated, arranged by client			
	Airfare			$1,200
	Hotel	$250/day	3 days	$750
	Travel subtotal			**$1,950**
	Estimated total cost to client			**$19,350**

Table 11-2. Sample budget for bid proposal

- ❑ What is your plan for paying bills when money is tight? Would you share it with your vendors and employees?
- ❑ Think of three things you could do to improve the way you set prices.
- ❑ Design a template for custom bids so that you can quickly create a proposal document and a budget spreadsheet the next time a customer knocks on the door.

12

Mastering the Budget Process

The more you know, the easier it gets.
—Anonymous

If you've come this far, then you know all the parts of the budget process, but there's still much more to learn. You can continue to improve your budgeting and management skills for the rest of your career. Here in this last chapter, we'll look at specific steps that you can take to learn more, succeed more fully in budgeting, and be more successful as a manager:

- Negotiating for your budget
- Improving your estimation skills
- Timing your budget preparation

Negotiating for Your Budget

One problem that every company faces is sometimes called *vertical communication*. There are barriers in talking with your boss, and when there's another boss above that, and then another, the folks at the top rarely have a good idea of what's really going on

"Just Fix the Problem!" "What Problem?"

One of my company's clients was a *Fortune* 100 investment bank with a very conservative reputation. The senior executives insisted that they really wanted honest status reports and an accurate report of problems from the lowest-level managers. However, the overall attitude of management at all levels was "Don't allow any problems to happen! Fix them before you need to tell me about them." The result was that lower-level managers, not wanting to face harsh criticism, would hide problems and try to fix them. But they often didn't have the money or authority to solve the problems.

I saw many of these difficulties when I trained lower- and middle-level staff in management. I asked for examples of problems and, wow, there were a lot of them! Major projects that the senior vice presidents thought were going along just fine were spiraling toward disaster. Ultimately, the bank was forced to merge with a much larger company and lose its autonomy.

at the departmental and supervisory levels. Executives have a limited picture and miss many of the details. At the same time, they must respond to pressures related to financial management, strategic plan, and the interests of the owners or stockholders. All too often, this makes it difficult for them to understand the financial needs of departments and respond well to budgetary requests from the bottom of the company.

If you want to get your budget approved, you'll need to understand the management structure of your company. What are the barriers to vertical communication? That is, what keeps your voice from being heard upstairs? What can you do to get the message through? Also, what are the company's attitudes toward money and the control of money and business operations? Once you can answer these questions, you can find out how to present the case for your budget. Keep these issues in mind:

- What adds value to the company?
- Who makes the decision? How could you get access to that person? What are that person's biggest concerns?
- What are the issues that matter most to the company?

How can you present your work plan and budget to address those issues?

- Is the company's decision process well defined?
- Are the company's criteria for making budgetary decisions rational? Or are the decisions based on narrow thinking or politics?
- How can you open a dialog, listen to the needs of executives, and get a chance to respond to them?

Keep all of these issues in mind as you prepare your budget proposal and decide when and how to present it.

Improving Your Estimation Skills

As we said at the beginning of the book, estimation is essentially careful guesswork. There are several things you can do to improve your estimation skills.

Year by Year

If you keep good records when you prepare your budget, you'll be able to remember your thinking when the next year comes around. You can check your thinking against reality by comparing the year's actual results with your estimate. As you do, here's what you can do to improve your skill for the next year. For each line item estimation:

- If your estimate matches the actual closely, good job! Do the same process this year. But don't just use the same number. For example, if your process was to interview customers, interview them again, rather than copying over last year's numbers. Be sure to take into account any changes from last year to this. For example, if last year you interviewed your five biggest customers, then don't interview the same customers this year. Instead, interview this year's five biggest customers.
- If your estimate was off in either direction, first ask what you missed. Check your notes. What made the actual results differ from your estimate?

  - If it was simply a calculation error, then change the way you make the calculation.
  - If it was something that could have been predicted, then change your method of analysis.
  - If it was a piece of information you didn't have at the beginning of the year, see if you can get that information this year.
  - If it was an outside event that you just could not have foreseen and there's no one you could have talked to who would have known, just let it go. These things happen: reality always gives us the unexpected.
- Don't forget the other parts of estimation. Review your choice of line items and see if you need to create new line items or split or combine existing items.

If you do this each year, you'll get better and better at estimating and making a budget.

Learning from Mistakes

As you start managing or gain greater responsibility as a manager, you'll make mistakes. We all do. There are many different views of mistakes. I think it's more valuable to solve the problem and learn from the mistake than to blame ourselves or get into debates about who's responsible for the error. I suggest the following steps:

1. Remember: the mistake is in the past. The issue is now the current situation, not how the mistake happened.
2. If necessary, do damage control. Take care of the situation to reduce the problematic effects of the mistake.
3. Solve the problem.
4. Take a deeper look and improve procedures so that no problem like this will happen again.
5. Share what you learned with others, so that everyone can improve the way they work.

Learning from our mistakes is not a one-time event. Maybe you've learned to keep good, up-to-date records of your trans-

CAUTION!

Don't Play the Blame Game

It's often far too easy when discussing variances between budget estimates and actual results to get into the blame game. Simple questions about the reasons for the variances can make people feel defensive—and soon the budget meeting becomes more about personal survival than understanding the fiscal situation and developing more accurate estimates. Be sensitive to the people behind the figures and focus on the future: two ways to avoid the blame game.

actions. Then two people leave your team in the middle of the busy season and things fall behind. There's no need to blame anyone. You all just do your best and start over. You can take this "no blame" attitude in relation to any error, whether it's an error in estimation, a failure to track expenses, or some other procedural mistake.

Timing Your Budget Preparation

All too often, we wait until there isn't enough time to prepare the budget for the next period or the next year. There's one good reason for waiting: the better figures we have for this year, the better basis we have for estimating figures for next year. However, we shouldn't wait too long. If we do, the benefits of having better actual figures will be less than the costs of not having enough time to do a good job. Here are two tips for making your new budget at the right time.

Preparing Templates for Future Periods

You can start some of your budgeting work a year ahead of time. When you finish this year's budget, immediately make templates for next year's budget. Simply add a column for the next year. Your column headings might look like Table 12-1. Save the spreadsheet and be ready to use it next year.

Item	2003 Estimated	2003 Actual	2004 Actual

Table 12-1. Column heads for a future budget

You can do the same for all of your spreadsheets and for all periods: months and quarters as well as years. For the items that have fixed future costs (such as rent on a long-term lease), you can even put the numbers in a year ahead of time. Keep these templates with your notes about creating the budget.

The 15-Month Budget

Some businesses use a technique called the 15-month budget that can really improve the quality of estimates and help businesses run smoothly.

Here's how to set up a 15-month budget:

1. Start two months before the fiscal year.
2. Make a 12-month budget for the fiscal year. At the same time, set up a template for the following year and fill in what numbers you can.
3. Make a very careful, detailed budget for the upcoming quarter (the first quarter of the upcoming fiscal year).
4. Use the quarterly budget from step 3 to create a quarterly budget for one year later.
5. Now you have an estimated budget for the next five quarters—15 months.
6. Three months later, create the budget for the 2nd quarter of the following year.
7. Every three months, create the budget for another quarter a year ahead.
8. When you get near the end of the fiscal year, check the entire next year's budget and make it as good as you can before you get it approved.

Smart Managing

Budget Time Frames

A 15-month budget is one version of a *rolling budget* or *continuous budget*. Some companies use a 12-month budget that rolls forward one month as each month is completed. That approach allows for greater accuracy, but it also means working on budgets every month. With a rolling budget appropriate to your situation, you can escape the confines of the year-by-year calendar.

There are a number of advantages of the 15-month budget.

- When you sit down to plan the year's budget, you've already got the first quarter done.
- It's very good for seasonal businesses. When you're thinking about this spring, for example, you're thinking about next spring as well.
- By getting into the habit of planning every quarter, instead of only once a year, you get better at estimating and planning.
- Each budget is effectively made twice: once, 15 months ahead, and then again when the year is planned and approved. As a result, the budget is more accurate.
- You have more opportunities to think about how the work is going when you make your work plans and estimates.

By working with a 15-month budget every quarter, you'll make estimation and budgeting a routine part of your management work, rather than a chore. This will give you better budgets and make it easier to bring your work plans, your team, and your budget together to succeed.

Manager's Checklist for Chapter 12

- ❑ What more can you learn about your company and the budgeting process to improve your negotiating position?
- ❑ What are the five things you might do if you find that your estimate from last year was off from the actual results?
- ❑ What could you do to have enough time to prepare budgets? What would the barriers be? Could you get the information you need in time? Could you convince others to work with you far enough ahead of time?
- ❑ Can you prepare templates for next year's budget now?
- ❑ Would the 15-month budget help your department?
- ❑ Make a list of three things you could do to manage your department's budget and three problems you need to

solve. Schedule time to make those six improvements within the next two months.

- ❑ Two months from now, check your list. If you've already done all six, make another list. If not, finish your first list and start another. Your work gets easier as you get better at it!

Index

Index

D